MA... PROCESS IT

Uncovering New Value in the Writer's Notebook

By Jeffery E. Frieden

MTME BOOKS

Published in the United States of America
By **MTMI Books**

Acknowledgments

This book would not have come together if it were not for several key people in my life who believed I was capable of writing down my ideas in a way others could understand and make good use of in their teaching.

First, I would like to thank my wife, Lindsey Frieden. When I first had the unexpected idea that I would write the contents of this book down in an orderly manner, my second thought was "how can I convince her that I need to leave her with an eight-, six-, and three-year-old for several hours at a time, sit and drink coffee while listening to jazz, and type out my thoughts?" This isn't the first crazy idea I have pitched to her in our marriage. After hours of listening to podcasts about self-publishing, I drew up a plan. I caught her at an opportune moment, went over the plan with her, and she was on board and very supportive. Whew! Thank you, Lindsey. You endure a lot and are a wonderful mother to our three kids. I couldn't have done this without your support.

The idea to write really came out of trying to explain what I was doing with my friend and colleague, Greg Mummert. I would get excited by what I was doing with my students and fumble through an out-of-context explanation that left more questions than actionable steps other teachers could take. He kept asking, "Are you writing any of this down?" At first I wasn't, but then I saw the potential, and started thinking through how I could put together a short book that explained what I was doing. I invited Greg to help me shape my writing in its early stages, as it was being typed on a Google Doc. Thanks, Greg, for all the feedback and helpful questions. This book would not have come together without you.

Another colleague who helped me shape my thoughts was Ashley Askins. We shared a prep period and would exchange ideas. I helped her with her master's course work and she would let me explain my ideas in fits and starts. We agreed that when she was done with her masters and that I was done with my book, that she would give it a try in her classroom. Thank you, Ashley, for helping me mold my ideas in the very early stages, long before there was even a thought of writing it out as a book.

Another colleague who helped in an immeasurable way was Laura Goodrich. I pitched her the idea that I would write a book. She was so excited! Her enthusiasm really carried me through the summer as I banged away on the keyboard between trips for coffee refills. Her enthusiasm was the energy source that kept me going when my desire was low. Thanks, Laura, you were a big help in getting this project off the ground!

I would like to give special acknowledgment to Robin Woods. She was my high school English teacher. Her influence has helped shape me as a writer and a teacher of writers stretching all the way back to my teenage years. At an opportune time, my parents were selling their house, and I paid one last visit to my alma mater while my parents were still living in the home I grew up in. I was able to connect with her and, since she is a published author too, I think that somewhere in the back of my mind, that's what brought the idea together that I could publish a book. Not only did she help in those subtle ways, once I announced my project to her, she gave me some extremely practical advice that has proved timely and immensely helpful. Thanks, Robin (though it is still a little weird for your former student to call you by your first name), you were a big help.

Gina Bernard, you have been a big part of the encouragement behind this book taking shape. You have been a champion for the cause for a long time. I have appreciated the feedback and the catching of the spelling errors. Writers (If I can count myself as one who has earned that title) need friends like you who care about their success and are willing to lend a hand whenever possible.

Keith Myers, my editor! You offered your professional services for free! My conscience wouldn't let me not pay you. I had to give you something, though it was a pittance compared to the value you added to this work. I appreciate you carving out the time. You're a charitable guy and a great friend.

Most of this was written at the Panera Bread on Limonite Avenue. I have to acknowledge how immensely helpful it was to have a space away from home, with coffee and Wi-Fi, where I could sit for a few hours and type. The staff there was great. And it was fun to run into Stephen Kish a few days a week too. Panera, your chairs are the best out of any local bakery and/or coffee shop.

I would also like to thank the readers of makethemmasterit.com and any of the related social media. You have made the journey interesting and entertaining. I don't know where I would be without all those 'likes' from Denise Bokman. I appreciate the support! I need it. You guys are the best!

Introduction

Writing has to be the most complicated subject to teach. Every student who enters our classroom starts somewhere different. Some enter with a high level of language skills. Others are still figuring out the basics. And, of course, there is every student in between. When we stand in front of them as teachers, we want to deliver the lessons we think will give us the most bang for our buck so we target those skills we believe are best for developing the group in front of us the furthest.

That approach is, to put it mildly, dissatisfying. I don't know about you, but I find it difficult to stomach thoughts like, "I just don't have enough time," "They need more than I can give," or "I can't individualize all my lessons for each student." Because I simply can't get to them all, I have lived a lot of my career with teacher-guilt. And I really suffered from an acute type of teacher-guilt: writing-teacher's-guilt. I know that you experience it too. It's the reason you're reading this. You're looking for an answer, some way to fix it, to make it better.

I can help. Really. Recently I experienced a guilt-free year of writing instruction. Yes, an entire year!

Before I show you how I was able to get past the self-blame of coming up short, let's take a look at a short list of my top frustrations as teacher of writing:

- Students wouldn't, or couldn't, integrate what was taught in a lesson to their writing.

- Students would think readers (usually me) were able to read minds and they would write too little.
- Most students' writing was one-and-done; they would almost never revise their work.
- When asked to revise, they would go for the easy fixes, like spelling and punctuation.
- And Students didn't learn from comments left on their compositions because they would NOT read them!

I still experience the frustrations on this list, but I have strategies and approaches for handling each and turn them into learning opportunities for my students. I now anticipate all of the behaviors on this list. Actually, I welcome them because they are where the learning happens.

Instead of facing these issues by "teaching harder," I changed my approach. I had heard about using a composition book a few times. I was first inspired by Kelly Gallagher when I attended one of his keynote presentations at a conference in Southern California. I quickly got my hands on *Teaching Adolescent Writers* where Gallagher outlines how to set up the Writer's Notebook. It was great! I followed that enthusiastically . . . for a couple of months. Then it fell out of use. Then I bought Aimee Buckner's *Notebook Know How: Strategies for the Writer's Notebook*. Another great book! I was reenergized and started again. And a couple of months later, it fell out of use a second time.

I went through this same cycle two more times, failing at each attempt. Then I quit. I convinced myself it wasn't for me and I walked away. Years later, I was at another keynote address with Kelly Gallagher. And there he was, holding up that same notebook, wowing the audience with all of the great learning he was getting out of his students. I made up my mind there: I was going to make my students keep a Writer's Notebook and I was going to get it right, all year long.

I did it! I got through a whole year with the notebook. I'll admit, it was hard. There were several times I wanted to quit. Gallagher and Buckner have great strategies, which I used, but what I needed in the middle of a long year was help: how to set up the Writer's Notebook, how to keep students interested all year, and how to get students to move from the notebook to more authentic writing. What I needed was logistics.

That is what I have put together in *Make Them Process It: Uncovering New Value in the Writer's Notebook*. It is a teacher's guide to teaching with a composition book. It's an approach that will get your students writing more than they ever have, developing revision practices that will mature them as writers, and teaching them grammar and language conventions at points that will cause them to stick. This book will come alongside you and help you through those moments when you are frustrated and help you decide what to do next with your maturing writers. It will help you see how you can get, not only better writing from your students, but a better understanding of how writing really works--that it is a process carried out in many steps with different, yet complementary, skills.

If you'll let it, *Make Them Process It* will change your approach to writing instruction in surprising ways. But here's the thing: you're already doing a good job. You're teaching your heart out and tinkering with your lessons to make them just a little bit better. I don't want you to change any of that. I just want you to change the order in which you do it. As you will discover in the pages that follow, writing instruction that sticks is about exercise, repetition, teachable moments and keeping every part of it low-stakes. Just like when I was learning the sport of water polo as a young man, the coach got me in the pool, told me to tread water and shoot, then helped me see what I needed to do to improve. In a similar way, you're going to have your students jump in and get writing, then coach them through their development.

C'mon. Let me show you how.

Table of Contents

Chapter 1 | Why a Writer's Notebook

Make Them Process Their Writing

Over the course of my teaching career, I have tried several different approaches to writing instruction. Most of them were mandated, or at least strongly endorsed, by my employers. And like any trial and error process, some things worked, and some things didn't. The first time I attempted to teach writing *via* a Writer's Notebook with my English classes, it was an instructional tool that I relied on for a time, but eventually I lost sight of how it fit into daily lessons, and I dropped it. In the spirit of being completely candid with you, I succumbed to this process several times.

Now, you may be wondering, "If this is something that you failed at multiple times, what changed to make you a believer?" The very short and simple answer was that "first taste of true success." That was the year I assigned the Writer's Notebook in the fall and had my students fill it with writing all the way through into the spring. That's what has me convinced of its power to enhance writing instruction increasing a writing teacher's impact.

What I needed in order to push through the trials and failures to get to that first taste of success was belief. Belief that students need to do more writing. Belief that students need to play with their writing. Belief that students need more choice in what they write. Belief that students need consistency in their writing practice. Belief that students need to revisit their writing often.

When I piled up all those beliefs and posed the question, "How can I take action on all these beliefs," the simplest and most all-encompassing answer is "the Writer's Notebook." It is a place for students to write a lot, a place for students to record their learning, a place for students to put into practice what they are learning about writing, and a place for students to return to their writing regularly.

One thing that I want to be absolutely clear about from the start, though, when I say, "Writer's Notebook: it's that simple," is the execution of the Writer's Notebook in your classroom as an instructional strategy is anything but simple. It's a challenge! One I struggled to take up myself. And that year where I had that first taste of true success, I had many moments of self-doubt, panic, frustration, and that feeling of being stuck. In those moments I would say, sometimes out loud, "I wish someone could show me what to do next!" And that's why I wrote this book.

If you're starting out on this journey, or hit a place where you're stuck, I want to help. I want be the person that can come alongside you and give you a timely piece of advice or word of encouragement in a way I didn't have. I also want to paint a complete picture for you, so you can see how this fits in the entire year.

I want to stay honest with you as you read this, so let me to tell you upfront that there are smarter and more inspiring teachers out there who have written about using the Writer's Notebook in their classes, like Aimee Buckner and Kelly Gallagher. I go to them for guidance about how to use this priceless instructional tool. And their strengths lay in presenting different strategies you can use within the Writer's Notebook, which can really help liven the notebook teacher's thinking in the middle of the mundane. But if you're like me, you need someone there to walk you through the process: how to begin, how to maintain, how to keep it fresh, and how to finish well. That's why I'm here. And that's what you will get in the pages to come.

Unburdened Writing Practice (And Depressurizing the Essay)

When I think about my first year of teaching, there are some cringe-worthy moments that come to mind. I know that I would wince if you asked me about that first essay I assigned. It was bad. If I could bring all my former students together as a group, I would issue a formal apology.

Writing is a complex activity. Academic writing is even more complex. Yet that's the point when most writing instruction tends to occur in classrooms where an essay is assigned. That's how I used to do it. The only times that I consciously thought about including writing lessons in my English classes were those times when the students were about to write an essay.

Think about it. If you're about to assign an essay and *THAT'S* when you want to introduce writing lessons, you are adding a lot of pressure to that assignment. I am guilty of doing this myself. I usually assigned many discrete writing activities, collect them, and give the students little to no feedback on their writing. Then, all of a sudden, WHAM!, I would say "essay" and pile on all the high expectations that good academic writing requires. "Your writing needs to look like this. You need to spell things this way. Make sure you only use the author's last name. Here's the format. Let's look at the 12 ways you need to quote a source. Remember to block out 90 minutes at the end of your essay to do a works cited page." And I haven't even brought up their level of motivation to write academically about a topic that was assigned to them, one they did not choose.

What was I doing to my students!?

What if there was a way to do consistent, low-stakes writing assignments throughout the year? What if they could learn some basics at the sentence-level? What if they could play with the skills they were learning, instead of being expected to "get it right" in their essay drafts? And what if they had some say in what they wrote about?

The Writer's Notebook is the perfect place for students to play, practice, mess up, and keep trying. It's a safe place to develop into a more mature writer. It's a place to learn, to evaluate, and to launch their writing into its polished form.

Think about this too: It takes tremendous pressure off of the essay and disperses it through the span of an academic year. Like the comical picture of a person trying to pack their closet into a suitcase for a two-week vacation, that's how I used to do essay writing instruction. In a way, using the Writer's Notebook gives the teacher and the student a more accurate perspective that helps them think through "how to pack" for that "essay writing journey."

A Playground for the Developing Writer

Activities are more enjoyable if you play. Just ask my three children. Whenever she gets the chance, my youngest will ask me if I can play with her stuffed animals that she keeps on her bed--she has a lot. Recently, I added a new element in our play time together where I sneak life-lessons in through stuffed animal dialogue. Not big ones, just little ones about parts of her life that we hope and pray she matures into. I might get the stuffed animals to share with one another, or maybe one of them will be mean to another one, and then that one will have to ask forgiveness of the offended party. She's having fun, but she is also practicing next-level maturity through her play. A win for her and a win for dad.

I try to take a similar approach with the Writer's Notebook. It is a place for students to play, without pressure, writing about a topic they are comfortable with. I have noticed that when the students get a level of say in the content that they are producing, without strict formats placed on them, they can write far more. They are more interested in watching their ideas unfurl on the page when no one is telling them how do it in the moment.

If you have ever flown Southwest Airlines, you know why play is important. Sure, they have attractive pricing for their flights, but there is some discomfort in choosing the airline. You have to take care of your own boarding pass, line up awkwardly when it's time to get on the plane, and the seats aren't the standard of comfort and personal space. But the people that work for the airline are professionals with an edge of humor. They play at work. And it makes the circumstance of dealing with a small amount of discomfort enjoyable. That's what allowing your students to play with their writing can do for them, bringing an ounce of fun to a process that makes everyone at least a little uncomfortable at each step.

Opportunities to Write in Various Modes

One element of my writing instruction that was missing

early on in my career was the importance of teaching students to write in different modes. If we were to go back and do a forensic investigation of the writing assignments from my first five years of teaching, you would think that there were only two modes: Exemplification and Argument/Persuasion. Since then I have come to appreciate at least touching on all the modes, which is easy to do with the Writer's Notebook, especially if it is broken up into weekly themes (more on this in chapter 3).

Last year, several weeks before I assigned an inquiry essay, I knew that I wanted my students to experience writing in several modes that might be helpful when they sat down to put their inquiry into words. I introduced three weeks' worth of themes, but instead of content themes, they were in modes: classification and division, cause and effect, and process analysis. Each week they were brainstorming short lists of topics to fit the mode in their "What Should I Write?" section--this is what I have the students title the pages where they brainstorm their writing, a title I have borrowed from Kelly Gallagher, which you can find in his excellent book *Teaching Adolescent Writing*.

In addition to the lists they were building, I was also prompting them a couple of days a week. For cause and effect, I had them pull out their phones and check their most recent text message and explain in 150 words how that message arrived on their phones. For a prompt and activity for classification and division, that I am slightly embarrassed about--but will shamelessly do again because of the writing it inspired--I had the students discuss, jot on Post-Its®, and then decide on what basis they would divide the topic "toilets in my life." I know, that topic stinks, right? But their engagement in that activity led to great conversations later when they were in the midst of their inquiry because I could refer back to it as an illustration of how to divide the subtopics of their essays.

Writing in the real world happens in different modes. And the texts that are worth reading, even the brief ones, usually include several. If we don't teach the students about the other modes, then they will think that writing happens in very confined boxes. But if their writing instruction opens them up to many different modes, styles, genres, or just different ways of putting ideas on a page, then they can gain an appreciation for all the ways they can express themselves in writing.

Instruction Paired with Choice in Writing

Students quickly gain comfort that they are not going to be judged harshly for playing, or taking risks, as they write their content. And after they have had a chance to play, I begin introducing mini grammar and craft lessons. I will take a simple sentence-craft concept, like how to write a complex sentence that leads with the dependent clause, and then challenge them to include one in their next entry. Or, after teaching them a very useful revision planning strategy (more on that in chapter 4), I might ask the students to go back to an entry and find a sentence they can replace with this element of craft, or two sentences they can combine.

Now, I'll let you in on a little secret: all that playing with writing the students are doing in their drafts is really creation of their writing curriculum. That's right. I am making my students create their own writing workbook! Sneaky, I know. But it works! And here's how: as the students play with writing, they are committing all kinds of language convention errors, which they will address through craft lessons where they will go back to those early drafts and revise into better ones.

If you have done sentence craft (or grammar) instruction in the past using worksheets or a textbook, you know you can barely hold the students' attention. And those handouts have the driest sentences. Boring! The students don't care, and they certainly don't place any value in fixing some other adult's vapid writing. But if it's their writing, it's different. It's personal. It's *theirs*.

With an inductive approach to writing instruction, I have them go back to their drafts and look for the good things they are doing, but I also have them look for the spots that can be improved. And there is far more student buy-in with this approach.

I will get to the how-to of using the Writer's Notebook with these methods, but for now it's important to highlight one more time that the students must be allowed to play as they build content, making their own choices. And not only in their initial draft, but in their revisions as well.

Helps Maintain Consistency in Weekly Assignments

As you can see, if you plan it out, the Writer's Notebook can be a showcase of all the different ways to write and learn about writing. At the same time, it can also be a nexus of consistency. I make the students write in there constantly. And I collect them for review (yes, I read them) on a regular basis, usually once every three weeks. These Notebook Checkpoints, as I call them, help with student buy-in because of their frequency. The students understand the notebook is not something that can be ignored or taken lightly, and so they invest more in their drafting.

If you're imagining stacks of composition books looming over you every three weeks, just breathe. Getting through their notebook is easier than you think. Remember, the students know that this is a writer's playground. As long as they are hitting some baseline requirements, like an established word count and writing in paragraphs, then they are going to get their points. And you get to know your students at a much more personal level.

I have been able to engage students at a deeper level because of some choice revelations they knew I would be reading: like how David, the extremely quiet student in my first period, let me know how playing the drums helps relieve all of his stress. I learn things worth celebrating with the students, like when they did well on a test they were dreading. And I also learn things that cause me to quietly pray for them. And there is the teenage drama because some students feel the need to unburden themselves about social tension at school, which, I have to admit, can be more entertaining than some of the best television out there.

More importantly, I have been able to get to know my students' writing habits, which makes it much more challenging for them to plagiarize another person's writing. When they have consistently written with a certain style and with a certain level of diction over three weeks, six weeks, nine weeks, then it becomes easy to see when things have changed. And I remind them of this fact as often as I can.

More than Just a Composition Book

I'm sure you're beginning to see how the Writer's Notebook is more than just a place for students to record daily bell work, while you take roll, before *the real* lesson begins. Actually, it's the opposite.

There have been lessons where, as I reflected, the students' authentic learning really only occurred in the Writer's Notebook that day. For my students it has become not just a place to write a lot of journal entries at the start of a class period, but a place for discovery, learning, reflection, and play. The Writer's Notebook is one of the best instructional tools, and is worth a great share of the teacher's, and every student's, time and energy as they work together to maximize its instructional value.

As you move into the chapters that follow, you will gain a clear vision of not only how you can use it on a weekly basis, but also how it can take your writing instruction to next-level revision practice and the authentic integration of sentence-craft lessons that matures student voice in writing.

Chapter 2 | Getting Set Up

Make a Place for Student Writing

So you have decided to get the Writer's Notebook into students' hands. Now what? There are a few things to consider before jumping in. This next section will describe what I do in setting up the Writer's Notebook with my students. This should be taken as a tool, not a rule. Each teacher's style and comfort-level should influence the instructional design of the notebook. But if you are looking for suggestions, let's begin.

The Notebook: Make Them Get a Composition Book

There are a lot of different types of journals and notebooks out there that can host student writing. If you manage to find a big brick-and-mortar bookstore, there is likely a section devoted to different styles of journal for every kind of person. These are neat, and I encourage us all to get one that fits us, but avoid fun journals for your students' Writer's Notebook.

Make them get a composition book. More specifically, make them get a 100 page composition book. Not 70, not 80. 100. Remember, you are going to have the students do a lot of writing and a fairly decent amount of writing about writing (completing lessons and taking notes). Finally, make it wide-ruled. No college-ruled composition books! Let me explain.

Now, if you are a high school teacher like me, you might be thinking "they need college-ruled because that's the direction they're headed." I don't disagree with you, but let's learn from my experience. College-ruled composition books are in scarcer supply--I have had students in the past who visited several stores just to purchase a one dollar notebook simply because I required college-ruled. Also, if we want our students to experience a certain level of comfort in developing their growing identity and skills as a writer, then they need space to work, mess up, cross out, overwrite, etc. A wide-ruled composition book is gracious in this regard. All things considered, the wide-ruled composition book is a better fit for everything you want to accomplish with the Writer's Notebook.

Once they have that 100 page, wide-ruled composition book in hand, then it's time to get set up.

Sections: Make Them Break it up

As a student, I have experienced the Writer's Notebook where I was only asked to write for the first 5-7 minutes of class while the teacher took roll or attended to other small tasks before instruction began. There was good in that. I tried out several humorous things, and I owe a measure of gratitude to that experience for developing my writing skills. I still have those notebooks too!

I want us to take a quick look one my entries from my junior year of high school to serve as a non-example, the type of notebook entry I would NOT accept from my students now:

> 5/18/94
>
> Do you think the rich are still above the law.
>
> Heck no! I think now-a-days the police men want to incarcerate rich people because their are 'jealas' of their riches. I know I would. But nonethe less the rich bribe and yes can get away with quite a lot. But not if I was a cop.

That's just silly. I make my students do more than this. The Writer's Notebook I am describing in this book, the one my students develop over their school year, is something with more levels of complexity and richer layers of design. It is intended to be the centerpiece of writing practice and writing instruction in the classroom.

You are going to make them draft a lot of entries and a lot of words with each entry. You are going to make them learn about writing, which they will record in the Writer's Notebook. You are going to make them revise their writing as they learn. And you are going to make them reflect on their writing after they have done a lot of drafting, learning, and revising.

To give you a taste of the kind of entries I expect to see in the Writer's Notebook I assign—which you will see is far more than what I was putting into my notebook entries in high school—here is a page from one of those notebooks:

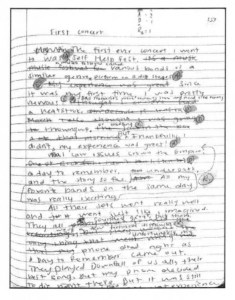

The difference is clear. Though I did produce *some* writing and develop *some* of my thinking in my Writer's Notebook when I was in high school, I want you to think about the amount and level of writing you want from your students. And if you're like me, the answer is **MORE**.

With that in mind, it is important to be clear at the outset about what goes into this composition book. Since this kind of Writer's Notebook dials up the complexity and intentionality, it is important to see that every page has a purpose. Here's breakdown I give my students for dividing up the Writer's Notebook into sections:

	WRITER'S NOTEBOOK SET-UP	
Pages	**Section Title**	**Purpose**
1-5	Table of Contents	List your titles of your draft entries only.
6-20	What Should I Write?	This is a section for brainstorming topics for your weekly independent writing assignments, or draft entries.
21-49	Craft	This section is designated for "craft" mini-lessons. "Craft" is defined as those things mature writers do, as well as fundamental grammar, usage, mechanics, and punctuation (GUMP). You will keep notes in about those practices in this section
50-199	Draft	This is where it all happens. You, the writer, play with writing on a daily basis, trying new things, and not worrying about "getting it right." This is a place for you to take risks and see how your ideas shape on the page. It is also where you will begin the work of revision before moving to a second, and maybe even a third, draft.
200	Rules and Guidelines	A reminder about how the draft entries should be formatted and what is expected from a "page" of writing.

I give this set-up to the students when they begin using the Writer's Notebook. It is important to communicate that there is a plan in motion. Now, for the rest of the chapter we'll take a deeper look at what goes into each section and why.

Table of Contents: Make Them Stay Organized

Since this is more than a bell-work composition book, it is important to stay organized. Remember, this Writer's Notebook will be built out slowly over the course of an academic year. It will be collected periodically and your students will need to know what you are looking at. And it is not going to be assembled in linear order because students will be flipping to certain pages to write entries, then flip back to an earlier part of the composition book to take notes, even further back to brainstorm, and finally, once they have completed entries or notes, they will record their titles in the table of contents.

It's best to have students keep an up-to-date Table of Contents. And keep it simple. I have the students jot down the page number and the title of their entries. I used to have them record the date, but that just complicates things. They often don't remember, or it brings feelings of guilt because they crammed five entries in the morning the notebook was due (more on this circumstance later).

Let me tell you why it is important to make them title their entries. When the students are practiced in titling their short compositions, they are much more confident and creative when titling their longer compositions, like multi-paragraph academic essays. And having them practice titling entries saves you from having to answer this question later on, "What do I title the essay?" I'm not sure if that annoys you as much as it does me, but when students get in the practice of titling their entries, almost all of those instances go away. This reason alone is enough to make the students keep record in a table of contents.

What Should I Write?: Make Them Brainstorm

To prompt or not to prompt? That is the question. This is especially true for the teacher who has been creating prompts for every entry for the last two months and the ideas have run out.

I used to think that I had to prompt the students each and every time they opened the composition book to write an entry. I am convinced that this was one of the main reasons that my early attempts at the Writer's Notebook failed. You shouldn't prompt them all the time. I have found that it's best that for every **one** prompt I give them, the students should generate **two** of their own topic ideas. That's why the words "Make Them" are in the title and throughout this book.

All right, you have decided not to be a control freak and you are going to let them come up with their own topics. The "What Should I Write?" section (pages 6-10) of the Writer's Notebook helps the students out. I did not come up with this idea. It came from Kelly Gallagher's *Teaching Adolescent Writers*. Basically, each page is a place for students to make lists of topics they can write about. Gallagher has his students start with something he terms "writing territories" and I have my students start there too. It's those topics, specific or general, that students have a lot to say about. I have them start with a list of 40 items. I show them my territories and talk through how I came up with those ideas. Then they start building theirs, which they don't need to complete in one sitting but should be completed by the first notebook checkpoint.

As the year moves on, you can use this section to tie in

with certain 'seasons.' On the next page you will find a list of examples you can make them create:

- 10 goals for this school year (*a good thing to get students to think about when school opens*)
- 10 things, or moments, that scare you (*good for when Halloween is around the corner*)
- 10 new beginnings (*use this at the start of the calendar year*)
- 10 reasons Valentine's day is the best (or worst)
- 10 ways to spend Spring Break
- 10 memorable moments (*ends the year on a reflective note*)

You can also have them build lists in anticipation of instruction. Here are some examples:

- 10 first experiences (*I used this before teaching the novel* Kindred)
- 10 public speaking fears (*given just before I made them present to the class*)
- 10 mistakes you wish you could undo (*good before* Romeo and Juliet)
- 10 laws you wish existed or could change (*C'mon,* Lord of the Flies)

The idea is to help guide them to prompt themselves, but allow them some room to take their thinking in a direction they want to pursue. It is also a way to respect them as developing writers. If we constantly prompt them, then we are allowing a lurking, unvoiced suspicion that their ideas aren't valuable, that the only things they should be writing about is what the teacher tells them to put on paper. And that is the opposite of what we want and expect as their teachers. We want confident, self-assured communicators who have enough maturity to take all the needed steps to produce clear, concise, and mature writing.

Making them prompt themselves will also relieve some of the pressure you put on yourself. You work hard. You have earned a little space to sit back and let someone else carry some of the load. Let them share in the burden of generating a topic. You will be surprised at how freeing this is. And the students will surprise you with the content they produce.

Craft: Make Them Notice Good Writing

When I was a young student, I had a few teachers that used daily oral language as part of grammar instruction. That's where they put up a sentence that's riddled with errors and the students are supposed to chase them down and wrangle them into their correct form. Theoretically, that's supposed to lead to students becoming better writers because they know the rules. That's been flatly debunked. It doesn't even warrant a citation here. Just plug in the words "daily oral language ineffective" to Google®.

Grammar worksheets where students practice a concept is better, especially if it is affirmative. Those are good for concept attainment, simply getting an understanding of the rules. But most grammar worksheets fall short of getting students to use the grammar they are learning in their own writing. Grammar instruction is one thing, their compositions are another. How, then, can we get students to transfer their learning about the rules of grammar to integration within their writing?

Including grammar instruction in the Writer's Notebook is the best, and most consistent, way to get new grammar into my students' writing and to review the concepts and skills they are taught on a regular basis. And there is no need to stop with grammar. My colleague and I use an acronym for when we teach sentence-level writing. It's GUMP. It stands for Grammar, Usage, Mechanics, and Punctuation. The blanket term we use is "craft," those moves a writer makes that produce clear, concise, and convincing communication.

There are many different approaches to craft and grammar instruction, so I won't prescribe one way or another here. If you have an archive of effective grammar PowerPoint® decks and great companion worksheets that you use with effective instruction, then you should continue to use those. I have found success using a more inductive approach to teaching craft lessons, where I put good examples in front of the students and ask them to tell me what they notice going on in the model sentences. Next they take notes and I ask them to imitate the craft they observed. And if you're interested in that approach, see Jeff Anderson's *Everyday Editing* and Kelly Gallagher's *Write Like This*, the section titled "Sentences of the Week."

Bottom line: the students need to take notes in the Writer's Notebook. And the lessons they are taking notes on, you need to make them use it in their entries, either in the first draft or in the revision process. I do NOT encourage teaching the lessons all at once. Instead, plan to integrate the lessons throughout each semester. Maybe you do it in bursts, where you do a few lessons in a row, and then allow time to practice. Or maybe you do one a week and give the students time to let that one lesson sink into their prose. Any way you do it, the students should be flipping back and forth from craft to the draft, creatively weaving their new learned skills to the writing they are committing to the page.

Draft: Make Them Write, Write, Write!

At this point, the students are set with ideas about how to prompt themselves, they have notes on key craft and grammar concepts that are really going to make their writing pop, so now it is time to write. That's it. They just need to write. And write a lot.

There are just a few considerations for the frequency and timing of their writing. Taking the year as a whole, I try to have the students write an equal share of entries in class and outside of class for homework. At the start of each semester, I have them begin by writing almost exclusively in class. I want them to get in the habit, and they will procrastinate (wouldn't you?), if you let them do it on their own. Plus, they need the consistent experience of having a calm place, where they can be alone with their thoughts, and find their voice as a writer. This takes time, so I give it to them.

If you have already done the math by my page count above, you'll see that I am anticipating that they will complete 150 pages worth of writing. That's not a stretch! They *really* can do that. My district slates 18 weeks per semester on the calendar. If I make them write in the notebook for 15 of those weeks, then they will do 75 entries per semester. 75 x 2 = 150. See! It's doable.

If you don't hit that number on your first go, don't worry about it. Take what you accomplished and build on it the next time around. So, let's say you get the students to produce 100 pages, each full with writing, by the end of the year. That's 100! Picture it. Your students are fanning the pages of their notebooks, and they are full of writing! It's an accomplishment for both you and your students.

Right now, if you're thinking about what you normally do

when teaching, and at this point I am asking you to add this to what you are already doing, it may seem daunting. Don't worry. I assure you, it's not. The Writer's Notebook is meant to be accommodating, graciously hosting the best of what you already do. In the next chapter, I will give you some ideas about how you can make the Writer's Notebook flexible enough to include not only the writing instruction you were already planning to deliver, but a way to house some reading instruction as well.

The Rules: Make Them Accountable

I want you to learn from my mistakes. When I first started the Writer's Notebook, I told the students to write for 10 minutes and whatever they accomplished in that amount of time was enough for me. I would tell them to write a page at home, and that's as specific as I would get. When I assigned entries to be completed at home, and spent less time on it in class, the students got lazy. They procrastinated. More than I would like to admit, my students would complete 12 entries the day it was due, writing like mad in their other classes before they had to submit their Writer's Notebooks to me later in the day.

And that's how I got Robert's entry on backpacks, pictured on the next page. It shows you what a twelfth grade student will produce clear expectations are not set for each entry in the writer's notebook. I overheard him discussing how quickly he wrote his entries, how he went fishing for topics from his friends. Between his desperate scrawlings (with ample space between words), he looked about the classroom deciding what to write about next. His eyes settled on that little bag students use to transport scholastic items from one classroom to the next.

Backpacks

92

In todays world we take advantage
of the usage of backpacks
They hold our whole
lives in them. A backpac
can be used for so many diffrent
situations. you can
use them at school, hiking, camping,
or just walking around.
A backpack holds
all of your electronics
and all of your
schoolwork. With
out a backpack
school would be
so hard because
you can't carry anything.
I appreciate backpacks
and I just
wrote about
this because I do
not know hat
else to write about
so I wrote about
backpacks.

At this point, I would like to share the two rules I have
for the Writer's Notebook:

1. Hit the minimum word count
2. Write in paragraphs

Word count will depend on what grade level you are working with. When I taught seniors, the minimum word count per page had to be 160 words. As a rule of thumb, make the entries at least 100 words, but you decide what's best for you and your students. The rule about writing in paragraphs was born entirely out of disgust with twelfth graders turning in page after page of monolithic compositions where they were not paying attention to where one thought ended and another began. I had to stop and teach the pilcrow and made them go back and find the spots where the thought shifted or changed.

As the year goes on, if I find they are guilty of other "sins of the page," then I will include more rules. Maybe it's not necessary to elevate the expectations to the level of a rule. Perhaps a guideline? For instance, after I have taught the students about the sentence structures and we have discussed sentence variety, then it may be time to flip to the back page and add a guideline about writing with varieties of sentences.

It's important to keep in mind that you make your expectations for their writing visible and that you keep encouraging your students to meet those expectations. In that spirit, don't be a stickler for the rules. For instance, if you have a student who is consistently meeting the word count, but is hit or miss with paragraphing, use that as feedback and ask him why some are in paragraphs and others aren't. They don't need to be penalized, but the rule leaves the door open for a teachable moment.

Before you have the students complete their first entry, flip to the very last page and have them write the rules or guidelines you set for the notebook. Refer to it regularly at the outset, and then taper off. That's it!

All Set: Time to Make Them Start Writing

Now that the Writer's Notebook is set up, you are ready to go. In the next chapter we will explore ways to run the notebook week over week and keep things fresh in the process.

Chapter 3 | In Process

Make Them Write a Lot without Losing Their Interest

I'm not going to pretend that it is easy to maintain an instructional practice for the entire year. All I have to present as evidence are my first few attempts at trying to run the Writer's Notebook. I treated it like a long jump instead of a marathon. I would get as much momentum at the start as I could, then I would leap to see how far I could get from that initial sprint. Instead, I should have paced myself and come up with strategies to get through.

The first time I was successful with the Writer's Notebook--meaning I made it through an entire academic year--I started with a commitment. Just before I made that commitment, I had the opportunity to hear one of my favorite authors discuss how important the Writer's Notebook is. He displayed some excellent student samples and I thought, "I have to give this one more try." But that time, before I launched the Writer's Notebook with my students, there was quite a bit of self-talk about how I wasn't going to quit, and I was going to see this thing through, etc.

I pumped myself up and then launched, with little more than advice from a couple of competent teachers, several failures to my name, and my self-proclaimed commitment based on the belief that this would be good for students. It turns out that was just enough to get me through. It worked. I made it! But I really could have used some help in the middle, especially when it started to feel like a slog. There were dark moments where I couldn't see what to do next or where I was going. Sometimes it wasn't enough, when I was in the thick of it, to hear, "But the research says that writing more causes students to blah blah blah." I just needed to know what to do next. Which is why I wrote this book: to help teachers get through a year with the Writer's Notebook.

In that spirit, let's lace up and get ready. It's going to be an endurance race. But you will have something I didn't on my first marathon: someone by your side. You know those tables overflowing with water cups for runners to stay hydrated? That's this book. It's a place you can return to throughout the year to cool off and get refreshed. I'm here. You've got this.

Now. To the starting line.

Teacher Led Prompts: Make Them Write

In chapter 2, I discussed the importance of making the students come up with their own prompts, and we'll get to that in a minute. There are times, though, that you will want to prompt the students. I try to use those times intentionally to maximize the impact of other areas of the curriculum. Let's take a look at some ways you can do this in your teaching.

1. Connect with student reading

When you are about to teach a complex text of considerable length, like a novel, this is a great time to prompt the students. Prompt them before and during the reading to help them manage their comprehension. Come up with prompts that are thematically related to what the students are reading. It could be that four of the five days in a given week, the students will be writing about their own topics of choice, and the other days you ask them to respond to a prompt you generate. I have found this is a great way to hook the students into the reading just a little bit more.

Another opportunity in prompting the students to connect with the book being taught is to help them manage their comprehension. When in the middle of a novel, I will ask students to list the three most perplexing things in the book they have read so far. Then I ask them to fill out the rest of the entry explaining their confusion and speculating on what could be causing their confusion, or what they think is really going on in the story.

On those days, it's not enough for the students to close their Writer's Notebooks and then open the novel to keep reading. I make them discuss their confusion. They have to stand up and move around, talking to different peers. This can help them see that they are not alone in their confusion, and they may even get some clarity. And having written it out prior to the conversation, they are much more articulate in explaining their point of confusion in the text.

2. Connect with upcoming lessons, projects, and presentations

There are times in the year when more complex assignments are approaching, like an essay or a presentation. Typically, in the past, I would just hand them a big, complex prompt on day one, and then we would hit the ground running. The Writer's Notebook has given me the opportunity to make the students participate in a more subtle mental preparation for the upcoming task. For instance, I may prompt the students with discussing their fears and anxieties. Or for catharsis, I may prompt them to write out their complaints with the project we are about to begin. Often this gives me insight into their misconceptions about these kinds of assignments. I also get a leg up on how to tailor a motivational message that speaks directly to their concerns about the coming assignment. But the key here is *they are writing.*

Also, you may want to find out your students' capabilities before this upcoming project. For example, you may want to know how adept your students are at uploading video into a designated web app. If you're familiar with a KWL chart--what do you **K**now, what do you **W**ant to know, and what have you **L**earned--the Writer's Notebook can function in the same way, but you can add in feelings. You can prompt the students with an entry where they share what they know, but also how they feel about their capability or what points frustrate them the most.

One thing that I hope you are seeing at this point is how the Writer's Notebook can be a gracious host to the other aspects of your curriculum. Yes, the Writer's Notebook acts as a stand-alone tool for instruction, but it can also be paired with other elements of your teaching. Why not have the students do prewriting for an essay in there? Just like in the game of basketball, a good jump shot is usually set up by a great pass.

Finally, students love the opportunity to double-dip for points. If you tell them they have to do pre-writing for a complex academic essay, they groan. But if you have been faithfully using the Writer's Notebook as a regular part of your class, after the announcement about pre-writing (with subsequent groans), imagine offering up, "But wait . . . you can do your pre-writing in the Writer's Notebook, and it will count as an entry." The scoffs will diminish and they will perk up. You are a savior. What looked like two assignments, in their minds, just became one! The workload cut in half!

3. Connect with inquiry and research

This is one of the more powerful elements of using the Writer's Notebook for informal writing. When I have my students in the midst of a complicated inquiry and research essay, the Writer's Notebook is a big help. I will prompt them to write about their understanding of the information they are researching, how it fits the prompt for the essay and how they might use the source in the essay--is it a primary support, secondary support, or a concrete illustration?

After I have made the students keep track of the texts they are researching, I can move them into metacognition where they write about how their opinion about the topic is shifting. At this point they can narrate or explain how their understanding of the topic has changed and become more refined and nuanced. This becomes an opportunity for the students to engage in meaningful class discussion as well. And since they have done a lot of writing about the topic, and their thinking about the topic, they will have a lot of valuable content to share in a class discussion.

4. Connect with seasonal events

Now that I have shown you how you can use the Writer's Notebook to expand the capacity of your students' minds and push them further in their thinking, let me tell you how the notebook can save your students from completely losing their mental function at key times during the year.

We all look forward to the holidays. Our students especially. But they lose the ability to function in class. You just want them to think through, fill out, and discuss this simple graphic organizer on the characterization of the main character of the story, but they are seemingly incapable of doing that. And you're not even sure you have the energy to be upset about it because you're already on vacation too!

This is where the Writer's Notebook can save everyone! Their energy is already pointing in a particular direction, just put a clever prompt in their path, and let them write what comes to mind. For me, I hate the effect Halloween has on my students. They completely lose their heads. But they are much more open to learning about "the use of details to set a mood" than any other time during the year. And, you could slip in a lesson about the sentence variety authors use to set that mood. Why get in the way of that natural curiosity by trying to strong arm students into caring about your favorite novel you teach? Just prompt them to write about something they are already thinking about. Turn it into a three-part lesson over three days and get three entries out of them.

I used to get frustrated with holidays, spirit weeks, and dances because they would disrupt my students' attention and pull them away from what I thought was clearly more important. After a few years, I realized this attitude is unproductive for everyone. If the students have energy going a certain direction, and you are not strong enough to stop it, then don't fight it. Instead, direct it. You and I know that writing can be about anything or anyone. Help your students see that. They will probably still balk and complain; they are young people after all. But after a few minutes, they will settle in and write. And they will probably be in the mood to share their writing with one another, so leverage that as well.

Choice: Make Them Generate Ideas

Now that you're getting a sense of when you should do the prompting, here are some tips on how to make students think for themselves. From a certain point of view, this is still prompting the students, though the result is a brainstorm of possible topics. Getting the students in the practice of coming up with their own topics is a good mental exercise for them. I'm sure you have experienced that most days students come in, sit in their assigned seat, and wait for you to tell them what to do. In my classroom, the Writer's Notebook is one place where the students, to a degree, set their own agenda.

In chapter 2, I briefly discussed the lists students can build in their "What Should I Write" section. Now, let me go a little further in depth about how to weave the practice of list building in throughout the year.

I want to touch on the "What Should I Write?" section briefly before I discuss having the students write in themes. In the section of the Writer's Notebook I am describing, the students will come to build lists, leave them, return to them, leave them, then come build more lists. It is a place for quick visits, a place for inspiration, a place to defeat writer's block. It's the Home Room of the Writer's Notebook. Stop by. Check in. Go forth. Don't have the students fill it all up at the beginning of the year; fill it as you go.

If you're the type of person that finds it difficult to work in a nonlinear manner, I apologize. I'm asking you to get used to the idea of leaving pages blank, skipping over them, then coming back later.

In the next section we'll take a look at how you can make the students generate their own ideas through weekly themes.

Weekly Themes: Make Them Stick with Something

There's something about themes, isn't there? Maybe it comes out of a natural desire to make connections and organize our thoughts in a certain direction, but thinking thematically is part of who we are as humans.

Thinking in themes is great for the Writer's Notebook for several reasons. It helps students to cut out the noise of a wild, wide open brainstorm and focus in a "fenced area," so to speak. Instead of constantly dealing with open-ended thoughts about what to write, the students have a space to go that is narrowed down and has boundaries.

Another reason brainstorming thematically helps is that it has the ability to keep things consistent for the students. If they have to jump from topic to topic, it can get quite erratic. Themes can have a calming effect and allow one to settle into a topic, which is a key component when preparing to settle in for a productive time of writing.

Finally, themes help keep the topic open enough to reduce writer's block. If the students have put together a list, and they don't like one of the items on that list, they can simply move on to another one that better fits their mood at the moment.

On the following pages are a three different ways to thematize entries for the Writer's Notebook.

1. Topical Themes

This is straightforward. For topical themes, I choose a topic for the week and have them build a list of ten things related to the topic in their "What Should I Write?" section. I decide. I inform. They list. Then write. Done. Just like that.

The only other layer of complexity I add is in choosing the topic. Using a similar type of approach discussed in the prompt section above, I take into consideration what we're reading in the class at the time, what lessons are coming up, and any seasonal events. That will help me home in on a theme that can hold student interest for several 100+ word entries, create at least a list of 10 possible subjects, and then select the ones from their list that they feel like writing about when they sit down to compose a draft.

2. Rhetorical Mode Themes

In my experience, my students don't get enough practice writing in the different rhetorical modes. Usually they are asked to do writing in the modes of exemplification and argumentation/persuasion. They write exemplification compositions when they are asked to do expository writing, like literary analysis in an English class. They come up with a thesis and then pile on the examples, explaining what each means and how it connects back to the thesis statement. When they're not exemplifying, they are arguing or persuading. But the pattern is fairly similar, at least in their production. They come up with a claim they want to prove or convince their reader about, then they pile on examples, and the occasional student throws in a rhetorical question for good measure.

You and I both know that there is a lot more to writing. The students are missing out on everything else that's out there. Many of the students don't get the opportunity to think through how to write comparison & contrast, process analysis, description, classification & division, definition, and cause & effect. They also don't get much of a chance to blend the modes into one composition either. But they could if a teacher will take just a little bit of time to work it into classroom instruction.

Imagine a student writer having enough know-how to think through the assignment in front of them and plan like this: "I think I will start with narration, then deliver my argumentative claim, present some evidence, then give a concrete description of what that looks like in real life, followed by more evidence, give my conclusion, and finish with the narration I started the piece with to wrap up my essay." That would be amazing! But how many modes do they know about? And how much practice do they have using writing in each so they can make decisions like in the hypothetical example?

Also, there isn't a whole lot of curriculum out there to support it. If you find such a curriculum, you're probably going to have to pay out of your own pocket to get it. Then let's say it arrives in your classroom, you will probably look at it and wonder how you are ever going to fit it in because the district pacing guides and school-wide strategies don't have any room for it. But with the Writer's Notebook, at the very least, you can give the students opportunities to explore and think through other modes of writing.

When I give rhetorical mode themes, I usually have to prompt them through each entry. Because the mode is *how* they write, and that's what I am making them focus their intellectual powers on at the moment, I need to provide them with *what* they are writing. There are many clever ways to do this. I gave two examples in chapter one, but since we're on that topic now, here's one more. If you were writing to the rhetorical mode theme of process analysis, you could ask them to write out the process they went through in the morning of deciding what to wear to school that day, providing reasons why for each step or decision point. Maybe they pick an area where they are an expert (this could be a list they build) and write a how-to for becoming an expert (you could show them blog posts of experts who do this, and then they model it).

3. Skills-Based Themes

For skills-based themes, maybe you have noticed that there is a particular deficiency in your students' writing and you are going to address it through instruction in the Writer's Notebook. This could be sentence-level, paragraph-level, or composition-level. For instance, you might have your "seven ways to write an effective essay introduction" lecture coming up. Why not kick off the week with the lecture, give them a prompt, and then have them practice writing each kind of introduction for their entries? If the intro is shorter than your allotted word count, so what? Let them get away with it. They will be grateful, which scores you a little cred with your students, and you get what you wanted: students trying out different ways to introduce an essay topic.

Regardless of which skill you emphasize, here's a bonus pro tip: make them engage in some evaluation and metacognition about the skill they have been trying on. Prompt them to rank which version they thought was most effective to least effective, then have them explain the ranking. After that, make them write a description of their thought process in deciding their top two choices: what were you thinking when you chose to use that method? How did you think that would make your writing better? Making your students write out their thinking in this way is another way to become aware of the choices writers make when they sit down to compose a draft, and it helps them see how they think through completing an academic task.

Include Writing Instruction: Make Them Learn Something & Make It Stick

If all you did with students was prompt them to write and have them write to themes, I imagine they would have a lot of content, but it would be a bit of a mess. The big idea that powers the Writer's Notebook is that students would get better at writing, not stagnate. I can think of no better place for instruction in writing than right there in the notebook itself.

At this point, I don't want to step on any toes. If you already have great writing lessons that help the students in powerful ways, I don't want you to change a thing. Well, maybe one thing: where the students put those lessons. Instead of taking notes on loose leaf binder paper, have the students take notes right in the notebook in the craft section.

There are two tremendous advantages to having the students keep their writing lessons in the notebook: storage and retrieval. First, they will literally carry the lessons with them all year. There is no mystery where the writing lessons are. But if you let them put it in a three-ring binder, there is no telling where it will end up. Second, since they will always have it with them, retrieval will be a snap. I have had very quick 30 second conferences with students when I have prompted them to include a certain skill in their writing, where the question posed usually is, "what do you mean, use a conjunctive adverb?" I respond with "what didn't make sense in the notes you took on page 32 of your Writer's Notebook?" Then the student sheepishly turns to the lesson and takes the opportunity to recall the skill.

Here are a few scope and sequence considerations for how you can plan your writing instruction with the available space in the Craft section.

1. Pre-load

When the academic year starts, there are certain things you already know the students will claim they are clueless about (why can they never remember the word "thesis?"). If you have taught your subject for at least one academic year, all the way through, take it from me, you already have a good grasp of the writing problems the students will bring with them when they show up in the fall. Why not start the year hitting those upfront?

I start my year with a mini-boot camp. I'll give the students a week to write without worrying about grammar, usage, mechanics, or punctuation (GUMP). Then I will hit a small stable of skills, what I think should be review at the point they came to me, one after the other in semi-rapid fashion. These will be the skills that I and my colleagues agree are bottom line. I may not even have them take notes on some of the skills, but may give them descriptive handouts, shrunken down to half a page, that will then be glued or taped into the Craft section of their Writer's Notebook.

2. Frontload

As the year goes on and complex assignments are on the horizon, in anticipation of developing the skills the students need, plan to introduce lessons *before* the students will need them. For example, if you have a research essay coming up--and you know that the students will be assessed on their ability to quote and paraphrase another author--work that into the Writer's Notebook. First, deliver an effective lesson on quotes and paraphrases that they capture in their Craft section. Then include two or three prompts for practice in the Draft section, using a text the students are currently reading.

For the lessons you frontload, let your guiding light be this: how can I depressurize the upcoming academic writing assignments? I don't think that I can emphasize this enough in using the Writer's Notebook, but you are saving you and your students' mounds of frustration by getting in front of the complexities that are implicit in academic writing. If your students have acquired a base-level understanding of a number of needed skills before entering the complicated process of crafting an academic essay, especially if it involves research, then you will be a much happier teacher.

Think about how much goes into writing an essay. First, they need a central, controlling statement, then they need to plan the support for that statement. After that, they need to plan an effective way to introduce that topic, but the writing can't be the same as the writing that supports the topic, after which they draft the body in rather specific ways:

transitioning, quoting, explaining, quoting, explaining, paraphrasing, explaining, concluding. Finally, they have to conclude their thought, but that's a different kind of writing too. Oh, and don't forget, we have to go back and look at how every single sentence they wrote was wrong, wrong, wrong! Seriously, who wants to put themselves through this?

Instead of scoffing at the amount of errors you're seeing in your students' writing, I picture something different for you. Instead, I want you to be able to say, "Wow, they really made a great attempt at introducing their quotes with power verbs!" It won't be perfect, but you will notice an elevation in their skills. Even before you get to assessing their writing, when they are in process, the questions they will pose will be of more effective. Instead of raising their hand and saying "I don't get it," they will be more likely to ask you questions targeted at their point of confusion: "Okay, I really want to use this quote because it supports my topic, but is it okay if I just write 'X said?'" Academic writing instruction can be so much smoother, and that's what I want for you and your students.

3. Download

As you are moving through the year, you will notice that there are errors the students are committing on a regular basis. This is the point where you will want to halt forward motion and point it out. If you picture your writing instruction for the year like a road trip, this is the time when you will want to get off the highway and gas up. Pause for a little bit to give a needed lesson. Maybe it will just be a quick stop and then you are back on the road, but taking a little time can really pay off for your students.

The trick is to save a little room in your craft section to fit these lessons in while on the fly. If you're using the amount of pages I prescribed above (about 30), then you'll want to save at least five pages for these kinds of lessons. If you're not sure how many to set aside, save a few more and assess your needs at the end of first semester. There is no hard and fast rule, but you will want to be flexible enough to include an on-demand lesson here or there.

Collecting, Reading, and Grading: Make Them Accountable

Ok. Take a deep breath. We're about to jump into the topic every English teacher loves to hate: grading. I know, I know. Nobody wants to talk about this. You may be tempted to just skip to the next section, but hang in there. It's not as bad as you think, and there are great benefits to reading and grading your students' notebooks.

First off, I don't know if I would really call it grading. I see it more as "checking in" to see if they did the writing entry count that you assigned. That's it. Keep it simple. Also, don't read every entry, if you don't have to. I make them keep a log sheet that they submit with each "Writer's Notebook Checkpoint" and they mark down the three that they want me to read because the students think those are the best representations of their writing. That communicates to the them that I am not going to read everything, and that's okay. But I tend to read more than three.

Also, while I'm on the topic, they are terrible judges of what you think will make interesting reading for you. I had a student mark that I should read an entry about Disneyland, which was just descriptive writing about different elements of the Magic Kingdom that he liked. Boring! I'm from Southern California; I have been to Disneyland and have seen The Mouse. I know what it's like. But sitting right next to the entry about The Happiest Place on Earth™ was one about how he doesn't try to get too excited about his birthday anymore. You see, his dad can't seem to remember it and they don't have that much money anyway. Mom's not in the picture, and dad's doing the best he can with the hand he's been dealt. Wow! That was much more interesting and compelling as a reader. And now I feel a little guilty for thinking his Disney entry was boring.

Reading the students' entries comes with certain benefits. First, you get a sense of what their writing needs are. In an essay, students work to hide errors; in the Writer's Notebook, they are right there for anyone with permission to see. Second, you get to know your students. A person may be able to hide themselves for a string of entries, but eventually that individual will start to show up in their writing in an authentic way. I have learned quite a bit about my students through what they have shared in their writing and this has allowed me to ask a little bit more about their lives. I was able to celebrate with some when they were writing about their successes, and I was able to express sympathies when learning about their tragedies. It helped connect me to their lives.

I tend to collect their writing after 15 entries, which is three weeks in my class. You can collect the Writer's Notebook whenever you want; you're the teacher. But if you collect more than 15 entries, you're going longer than three weeks without getting eyes on their writing. And if you're collecting it in fewer than 15 entries, you will have to collect the notebooks a lot more often. A final word of caution: if you teach five sections of a subject like I do, then stagger your submissions. Don't collect five classes at once. It will feel overwhelming. Split it up three classes this week and two the next.

There, now that wasn't too bad, was it? You don't have to grade everything. You don't have to read everything. But when you do, you will be given an opportunity, in a small way, to enter their worlds. You will see a different side of your students, a more vulnerable side. Trust me; it's worth it.

Considerations

This probably goes without saying, but when students are given the opportunity for freedom in their writing, they have more opportunity to open up about some of the messiness of their lives. In some cases, they may reveal some of the dark corners of their experience and some may be in real danger of being hurt or hurting themselves. And, though extremely rare, some may have plans to hurt others. As a teacher, get to know your state laws about *what* should be reported to the authorities and *when* you have reasonable cause to do so.

In the state where I teach, I am a mandated reporter. I understand that using the Writer's Notebook with my students opens me up to more opportunities where I may uncover some unwelcome news or perspective. For me, I look forward to the opportunity to work with students to get the help they need. And if the students are willing to write about those parts of their lives that few others get to see, in my mind it is the same as any student developing enough trust with any teacher or staff to share what's really going on this young person's life.

If you have any concerns about this, then do a little bit of research about your state's requirements for reporting about abuse and when students are presenting the signs of being a danger to themselves or others. Better yet, you may consider asking a counselor or assistant principal at your school.

Chapter 4 | Revision

Make Them Look at Their Writing a Second (or Even a Third) Time

Up until this point we have been looking at ways of putting student writing *into* the Writer's Notebook. Let's now turn our attention to how to get improved writing *out of* the Writer's Notebook. As you and your students move from drafts into the stage of revision, it is important to remind them regularly that writing is a process.

The hidden curriculum here is to get the students to completely reject the idea that their writing is a thing that is ever *finished*. We writers are never done. There is just the current draft and the deadline. That's it. The students need to appreciate that their writing can always be changed, modified, and tinkered with in order to make it just a little better.

As I have made the Writer's Notebook the centerpiece of writing instruction in my classes, I have come up with a process for revision that I take my students through on a regular basis. Just like all the other writing the students do in the notebook, this practice is low-stakes. It is more about learning the process, the moves, and the rhythm of moving from draft to draft so that when they get to the high-stakes, academic writing assignments, they have already been freed up mentally to focus their learning on the complex skills needed for academic writing.

This method of teaching revision has quite a few moves. What will really help us as we move through this section is if we have a map of sorts. Let's call it the "Make Them Revise It" map. Take a look:

THE "MAKE THEM REVISE IT" MAP	
Step	**Task**
1	Write a number of entries in the Writer's Notebook
2	The students choose an entry to revise
3	They plan their revisions by annotating their chosen entry with the revision tool you have chosen
4	The students use the plan to write the next draft (consider using the Meta-Margin)
5	The students highlight the changes they made when writing their second drafts
6	The students hold writing conversations about the changes made, taking notes on their thinking.
7	The students record their metacognition and make it visible, writing it in the margin of their second draft.
8	The students submit their work.

As you read each section, I will highlight the steps from the map that correspond with the information presented. Think of this as the "you are here" function seen on the large maps that can be found at the mall.

The First Read-Through: Make Them Plan Their Revisions

Before the students leave the pages of the Writer's Notebook and begin a second draft, they need to have a plan for how they will improve their writing. There is no shortage of revision strategies hovering out there in the internet ether. A quick Google® search and ten minutes of haphazard clicking will show you that there are plenty of different ways to approach how to plan for revision. There are also plenty of acronyms as well: COPS, CUPS, C-SCOOP, STAR, STOP, etc. Many of them are great! I encourage you to explore the available options and find the one that works best for you.

For me, I have settled in on one easy-to-understand tool for revision that helps students catch the problems they are seeing in their own writing: RADaR. It stands for Replace, Add, Delete, and Reorder. I like this tool because the students grasp it quickly and it lends itself to silly sayings that stick in the minds of young learners. For example, when they finish an entry or a draft, I will say, "Okay, it's time to run our writing under the RADaR." Or I may quip, "Did you use your RADaR to spot the bogies, the enemies of your better draft?" It's cheesy, I know, but it allows me to bring up the tool in fresh ways. It helps because I make the students use it frequently.

I first discovered this tool when reading Kelly Gallagher's *Write Like This: Teaching Real-World Writing Through Modeling and Mentor Texts*. It is further developed in Prentice Hall's writing program that Gallagher co-wrote with Jeff Anderson (2012) named *Writing Coach*. I'll leave it to him to give you a detailed explanation for how the revision tool works. What's important at this point is that you choose a tool that you use consistently when having the students proofread their own writing.

One more consideration. When you first hand the students your revision tool of choice, I suggest prescribing the extent that they use the tool. For instance, with RADaR, I make my students do a certain number of each element--if they aren't forced to practice, some will never make the attempt. In a 150 word composition, I will have the students make 2 replacements, 2 additions, 1 deletion, and re-order one element, at least. They may do more, but the bottom-line is that they need to get into revision mindset, and sometimes they must be dragged into it kicking and screaming. And that's okay; it's an opportunity for them to learn. I have had great revision conversations with reluctant revisers who were stumped at what to do, but when I read through their first draft alongside them and made suggestions based on what was there, the students would light up at the potential they had on their page.

Here's where we are on the map:

THE "MAKE THEM REVISE IT" MAP	
Step	**Task**
1	Write a number of entries in the Writer's Notebook
2	**The students choose an entry to revise**
3	**They plan their revisions by annotating their chosen entry with the revision tool you have chosen**
4	The students use the plan to write the next draft (consider using the Meta-Margin)
5	The students highlight the changes they made when writing their second drafts
6	The students hold writing conversations about the changes made, taking notes on their thinking.
7	The students record their metacognition and make it visible, writing it in the margin of their second draft.
8	The students submit their work.

When students use the revision tool in their Writer's Notebooks, I give them a procedure for how they will mark their page. When they mark the page, they are making their thinking visible, which will really help them transition from the first to the second draft. Also, just like the students will write more pages than you will ever read, you should feel free to have them proofread more pages than you plan to make them revise. Just because they proofread it and marked it up, doesn't mean that they you have to have them go forward with it. The practice of thinking through a revision is valuable in and of itself.

The Second Draft: Make Them Better It

I know we just looked checked in with the map, but let's take a look again. The next page shows us where we are:

Step	Task
	THE "MAKE THEM REVISE IT" MAP
1	Write a number of entries in the Writer's Notebook
2	The students choose an entry to revise
3	They plan their revisions by annotating their chosen entry with the revision tool you have chosen
4	**The students use the plan to write the next draft (consider using the Meta-Margin)**
5	The students highlight the changes they made when writing their second drafts
6	The students hold writing conversations about the changes made, taking notes on their thinking.
7	The students record their metacognition and make it visible, writing it in the margin of their second draft.
8	The students submit their work.

Before you have the students dive in, let's consider a few approaches the students can take in their second drafts. Each consideration is an opportunity for you, as the teacher, to think through what would benefit your students the most.

1. Access to Technology

Depending on the resources you have available, you could move this next step from ink and paper to a word processing application. I have the advantage of working at a school that has access to laptops and a Google® domain, which gives the students access to G Suite® where they can learn word processing online. I use their second draft as an opportunity to move their writing into word processing because, in my experience, most students are not gifted word processors.

And if you have access to word processing technology, I encourage you to use it at the step of writing a second draft. Why? Get used to me saying this: take the pressure off! Typing up a 150 word draft gives your students a low-pressure opportunity to develop typing skills and better awareness of your prescribed formatting, MLA in most classrooms. If the students learn these little skills ahead of the complex academic writing you have planned down the road, this will free them up to learn, accommodate, and consolidate how to word process before they have to type a multi-page essay. And *when* you are teaching a multi-page essay, instruction really slows down every time you have to remind them how to double-space, the order of the heading, or hit tab once to indent. And for my sanity's sake dear students, stop hitting space bar *ad nauseum* until it appears like your title is in the middle. It's not!

2. 'Learning the Process' is the Greater Need

If you don't have access to technology, then use binder paper and a pen. The greater benefit to their growth as writers is making the students compose a second draft. They need many opportunities to gain experience with this part of the writing process. They need to take an idea, churn out a number of words developing said idea, revise it, put out a better version, then even go back again to make it that much better (more on this when we get to publishing in chapter 6). Also, making them produce a second draft leads them to the step where they *think* about their own writing, which I am convinced is the most important aspect of my writing instruction.

3. Anticipation of Metacognition

Whether or not you are using an electronic device or paper and pen, I suggest you consider what you have the students do with the second draft after it is written up. For my students, it's not enough for them to just submit a second draft and leave it at that. They need to evaluate the effectiveness of their decisions at the stage of revision. If a teacher merely collects the second draft without having the students evaluate their choices, it puts that teacher in the position of thinking through how to assess and score the writing. As you read on, you will see how I make the students assess and score their own second drafts, so you don't have to. But to help us get to that point, I would like to introduce you to *The Meta-Margin.*

When I have my students write out a second draft, they do it on a page that has a "Meta-Margin." Simply put, the students make room for a 2.5 to 3 inch margin on the right-hand side of the page to make space for metacognition. If you're familiar with Cornell Notes, visually speaking, I ask them to place the large margin on the opposite side of the page. After they have written out their second draft on to the left of The Meta-Margin, they go back over their draft and explicitly write out their thought process that led to the changes they made.

I bring up the Meta-Margin here in anticipation of how it will be used. At this point in the revision process, the Meta-Margin is a blank space. We'll get to the ins-and-outs of how to the students will make use of this space after they have marked up their second draft.

Writing Conversations: Make Them Talk about Their Choices

Before we get into steps 5 and 6, I want to point out that making your students talk about their revisions is not as crucial as the metacognition in step 7. If you feel unsure or uncomfortable about how to guide students through holding writing conversations in your classroom, feel free to skip to the next step. Perhaps after you have taught the other steps in the revision process, and developed some familiarity with the steps, you can come back to this one as a way to add another layer of maturity for your students.

That being said, I do invite you to consider hosting writing conversations and continue reading this section, even if you won't be practicing it your first time through. If you train your students to be able to comment well on one another's drafts, it will relieve you from having to look at each and every paper produced in your classroom. Also, this is the level of maturity we should come to expect from our students—that they can slow down, take a good look at their a classmate's writing, and be able to make a mature comment on their developing ability.

So, let's see where this would fit in to our teaching and try to make space for it. And to do that, let's check in with the map again on the next page.

THE "MAKE THEM REVISE IT" MAP	
Step	Task
1	Write a number of entries in the Writer's Notebook
2	The students choose an entry to revise
3	They plan their revisions by annotating their chosen entry with the revision tool you have chosen
4	The students use the plan to write the next draft (consider using the Meta-Margin)
5	**The students highlight the changes they made when writing their second drafts**
6	**The students hold writing conversations about the changes made, taking notes on their thinking.**
7	The students record their metacognition and make it visible, writing it in the margin of their second draft.
8	The students submit their work.

For this part, I recommend using highlighters. This is a reason why I like RADaR as a revision tool; it covers many of the elements of revision, and those elements fit well in four categories. Most highlighter packs come with four colors of highlighters. With their Writer's Notebook open to their marked up entry, and their second draft sitting next to it, make the students read their second draft and mark it where they made the changes.

At the conclusion of this step, you should see their first draft marked up with notes. Next to that you should see their second draft highlighted where they made the changes.

As you move to the next page, what you will see are the papers that should be on their desk when they are done with step 5.

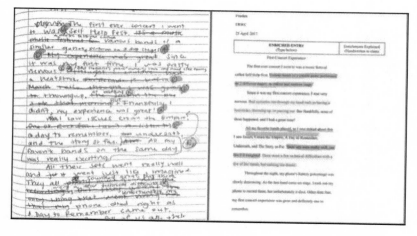

Here's the highlighting procedure I make the students use:

- **Replace** = yellow - they liked the original idea in their writing, but they reconsidered how they packaged the idea by replacing what they initially wrote with a new wording.
- **Add** = green - it's new, why not green?

- **Delete** = pink - they *stopped* using it, like a stop light, and pink is light red, right?
- **Reorder** = blue - the other colors were taken.

After they mark up their drafts, have them swap with a partner. Then they read one another's new draft *with highlights*, completing a read aloud where the author listens to the reader and asks a couple of follow up questions. In my class they will use the Revision Read Aloud guide to assist the conversation (See Appendix C for the handout). One partner will read aloud the other's 2nd Draft Entry and will say their thoughts out loud as they are prompted by stems on the Revision Read Aloud guide. The author of the second draft will record the thoughts spoken by her or his reading partner. After reading and thinking aloud, there are two follow up questions the author of the 2nd Draft Entry will pose to the reading partner and record what she or he says. The pair will switch roles until they have completed the activity.

Here's what they will need for step 6, when they hold the writing conversation:

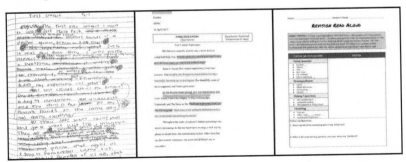

Essentially, in this exercise the author of the 2nd Draft Entry is taking notes on the thoughts of a person who is reading the author's work aloud. For students who don't think much about the moves they make when they write, this will push them to go back to their own words and key in on those parts they revised. This puts the young writers in a position to test their thinking--they believed, at some level, these revisions would make their writing better, and now they will know how accurate their thinking was.

After the students have completed the Revision Read Aloud, they are ready to make their metacognitive thinking explicit in the margins of their second draft. If their second draft is formatted with the Meta-Margin, they will have space to write out their metacognition.

Metacognition: Make Them Explain Their Thinking

After planning their revisions, writing the second draft, and talking about their revisions through a guided conversation with a classmate, the young writers are ready to make their thinking about their revision choices visible. That's step 7 on our map:

THE "MAKE THEM REVISE IT" MAP	
Step	Task
1	Write a number of entries in the Writer's Notebook
2	The students choose an entry to revise
3	They plan their revisions by annotating their chosen entry with the revision tool you have chosen
4	The students use the plan to write the next draft (consider using the Meta-Margin)
5	The students highlight the changes they made when writing their second drafts

6	The students hold writing conversations about the changes made, taking notes on their thinking.
7	**The students record their metacognition and make it visible, writing it in the margin of their second draft.**
8	The students submit their work.

For me, as their teacher, *this* is the part of the process where I focus on assessment and scoring. I'm not as concerned with reading their second drafts, but rather *the thinking that led them to produce their second drafts*. If I can get the students to think through their writing choices in low-stakes assignments, when they get to the more complex and academically rich writing they will be asked to do, they will have built-in mental habits that will carry them through revising their multi-page essays.

The only difference between this step and the conversations with a classmate is that the students are writing out their thinking in the margins of the second draft. This is why I make room for The Meta-Margin, so they will have enough space to thoroughly write out their metacognition. The students spread out their materials--their original draft in the Writer's Notebook annotated with their plan for revision and their second draft--and they highlight the elements they changed from one draft to the next. Then they explain their thinking in the margin.

When you turn to the next page, you will see a sample of what students produce when they are tasked with making their metacognition visible.

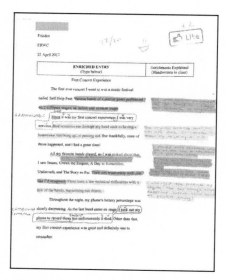

In my class, I have some sentence frames to guide them. Again, I use RADaR, so the frames are organized according to that method of revision. I get the students to think in two categories: surface and deep level revision. There is a complete list of sentence frames in Appendix D, but to give you an idea, here is a look at the frames I have developed for students to explain replacements they have made between drafts:

REPLACE (RP)	
SURFACE-LEVEL REVISION	**DEEP-LEVEL REVISION**
Better word ➤ "_____ was a better word than _____ because . . ."	**Changed the focus of the writing.** ➤ "I replaced _____ with this text because the first draft communicated _____ when really I want to get across that . . ."
Clarity - Made the sentence clearer ➤ "Replacing the word/phrase _____ with _____ made the sentence clearer because . . ." ➤ "My original sentence was _____, so I made it clearer by . . ."	**Clarity - Made the whole piece clearer** ➤ "I replaced my first example/story of _____ and replaced it with this example/story to make it more clear that . . ."
Too abstract/concrete ➤ "_____ was too abstract, so I replaced it with _____ which better specifies . . ." ➤ "_____ was too concrete, so I replaced it with _____ which broadens the idea of . . ."	
Avoid repetition ➤ "I replaced _____ with _____ because I already used that word/phrase in . . ."	

You should adapt these to fit the need of your classroom, especially if you are using a different tool.

I also have a scoring guide checklist that the students fill out as they move through the steps of making their thinking visible. An example and more information are provided in appendix E.

Practice: Make Them Revise Again and Again (Depressurize the Revision Process)

If you are considering taking full advantage of implementing this process, it's most likely new to you. And if you're like me, doing new things can be intimidating, especially something you can't clearly and distinctly picture. To help remove some of the anxiety, I have put together PowerPoints that will help you through the process. If you believe that it would be a help to you, you may download them and use them. You can find them at https://makethemmasterit.com/mtpi-dropbox/. Feel free to modify the slideshows to fit your style and personality. I simply ask that you do not change content of the final slide.

If you're at this point with your students, you have taken them through the revision process one time. But that is not enough. They need to keep doing it. Make them run through these revision repetitions as often as you can. Why? For the same reason I keep repeating: it's a pressure release valve for the more complex writing tasks in your classroom

When you give your students of writing a complex academic essay, and they are moving into the revision process, wouldn't it be great if they had really good revision habits built-in to their approach? Imagine how it could free you up from feeling like you have to teach them at every step of the academic essay. Then you could get to the place where you would have intelligent conversations with your students about content choices in their writing. They won't say, "I don't get it" or "What am I supposed to do again?"

Since you're only going to be paying attention to how the students are making their thinking visible, grading these assignments will be a snap. This means that you can do it again and again, at a pace you think is reasonable (once every week? every other week?). In my classroom, there is a designated day of the week for this. We step out of the flow of our regular curriculum and make room for these reflections. Then we move back into the flow.

At the end of this book are two resources that should give you a clear picture of how to implement this regular revision practice into the overall design of your curriculum and lesson plan calendar. Appendix A will guide you through how to integrate the Writer's Notebook, including revision, into your calendar.

And to get a more concise picture of how this can look in a three-week side along unit, go to Appendix B. There I will walk you through the steps of making revision a regular part of your instruction, without causing too much disruption to the rest of your curriculum. This is also helpful if you are picking up this book late in the academic year, and you like what you're seeing, want to see it in action, but you're not sure how to make it fit with the time-frame you have left. Following the plan in Appendix B can give you a taste of what the whole year could be like.

Chapter 5 | Sentence-Level Craft

Make Them Try Something New

Remember all those craft and grammar lessons the students have been entering into the Writer's Notebook? Those weren't meant to sit merely as a reference for the students who felt the need to review them. Those lessons are there for the students to revisit so they can integrate the skills into their writing. A great place for the students to do this is in their second draft.

Until this point of the book, *Make Them Process It* has been a practical guide in implementing more low-stakes writing into the classroom and how to draw out opportunities to practice revision. But I'm going to take a brief pause to discuss pedagogy. More specifically, *when* to teach grammar and writing conventions in your classroom. In the 1980s George Hillocks completed a famous meta-analysis studying the effects of traditional grammar instruction. As part of his summary, he wrote, "School boards, administrators, and teachers who impose the systematic study of traditional school grammar on their students over lengthy periods of time in the name of teaching writing do them a gross disservice that should not be tolerated by anyone concerned with the effective teaching of good writing." He also made plain that, "The study of traditional school grammar (i.e., the definition of parts of speech, the parsing of sentences, etc.) has no effect on the raising quality of student writing." Here's the gist: teaching grammar before and separate from writing is not an effective way to improve writing.

Hillock's insights and my experience teaching grammar are why I have completely flipped how I sequence grammar instruction. Instead of grammar before writing, in my classroom it's writing before grammar. Students are much more attentive to grammar lessons when those lessons directly apply to their own writing. In the case of the Writer's Notebook, when the students write 100 or more words of prose, they are framing the composition toward a reader of their choosing (whether they are conscious of this or not). When the students are tasked with applying grammar language conventions *after* they have written a first draft, they get the opportunity to integrate a skill that fits their composition and better communicates a point to their audience. *This* is grammar instruction in context.

Growing up, I was taught grammar before writing. I was taught the rules, given daily oral language exercises, and I had to diagram sentences. I have tried these approaches in my teaching, and I got the same results that all the research suggests: grammar instruction before teaching writing does not have a positive effect on student writing. But when I moved that same instruction into the revision part of the writing process, it did have a positive effect. The key detail to notice here is not that I changed my grammar instruction in a new or revolutionary way. I simply moved that same instruction from the beginning to the end of the process and repackaged the instruction to fit the context of the Writer's Notebook.

Let me tell you some of the things I started seeing in my

classroom. Students saw the application to their own writing and they learned how to integrate language convention skills into their prose. My students even developed curiosity about grammar and how to phrase their sentences. They began asking me pointed questions while they were drafting. This was the kind of learning behavior I had dreamed of seeing in my students before entering the profession.

There is a little bit more to consider than moving the instruction to a different point in the process. The lessons are shaped differently, and you will need to constantly bring students back to their drafts. This chapter will guide you through how you can add grammar and language convention instruction to the revision process. First, let me show you what it looks like.

Painting the Picture: What It Looks Like to Make Them Try Something New

As the semester unfolds, and the craft and grammar lessons are stacking up in the Craft section of the students' Writer's Notebook, I will highlight particular skills that I think can push their writing to the next level of development. And to that end I add sentence craft skills to their scoring guide checklist (see Appendix E), which means I will need to see it in their second drafts. Since grammar and sentence craft are clearly defined and objective writing skills, I hold the students responsible for assessing their own work. That's right. I make them grade it!

For example, early on I teach the students the four sentence structures: simple, compound, complex, and compound-complex. Once they can identify the four sentence structures, it's time to challenge them to apply their knowledge. And as anyone who has taught grammar can tell you, there is a large gap between the students being able to recognize a grammatical structure on a handout and being able to intentionally write their own sentences using their knowledge.

One element of craft I draw their focus toward is writing complex sentences that lead with a dependent clause. Borrowing the concept from Jeff Anderson--while putting my own little spin on it--I refer to these sentences as SubCon openers.

When the students write a SubCon opener, and they are asked to identify it and label it in their own writing, here's the procedure I make them use for marking up their second drafts:

SubCon Opener: (5 pts)
- ☐ Underline the opener.
- ☐ Label the **subordinating conjunction** by writing 'SubCon' above it.
- ☐ Circle the punctuation mark between the opener and the independent clause.
- ☐ For all clauses in the sentence,
    - ☐ label the **subject** with an 'S' above the word(s) &
    - ☐ a 'V' above the **verb**.

I use the checkboxes so they can check off the completion of each step (see the other sentence-craft checkboxes in Appendix E). Also, you will notice that these elements should be fairly easy to recognize. But when a student presents me with their second draft, and it's marked up, I can instantly see if they understood how to write this type of sentence. If they misunderstood one or more elements I can pinpoint exactly where the misunderstanding occurred.

Here's what it looks like on the page of the second draft:

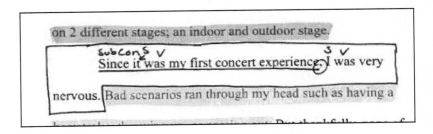

on 2 different stages; an indoor and outdoor stage.

SubConS V   S V
Since it was my first concert experience, I was very

nervous. Bad scenarios ran through my head such as having a

Let me interrupt these instructions with a quick story that shows the value of this practice. Last year, through using this procedure, I learned that many of my seniors struggled in their understanding of verbs. Many were not sure what a linking verb was, or what it did. If I hadn't structured their revising lessons this way--hadn't made them go over it a second time to explain their thinking, and a third time to show off their sentence writing prowess--I would have sent many seniors off to college without a functional understanding of a linking verb. That's frightening!

When giving the students instructions for including sentence-level craft in their revision, I only require two sentences. As the students continue to add sentence craft lessons to their notebook, their repertoire will expand, but the practice of including elements of craft and grammar needs to remain a manageable number. Besides, real-world authors and writers don't sit down with a quota that details how many complex sentences, quote introductions, or appositives they need to include in a piece they are writing. They write to communicate clearly with their audience. And yet this practice is great for developing writers because it gives them a chance to practice a new skill, to try it on and see how it goes.

Now that you have a picture of what this looks like, in the

next section, I will show you how to blend it into the students' revision process.

Include With Revision: How to Make Them Add This Practice

Before adding in this practice of increasing sophistication of your students' sentence-level craft, make sure they have developed their metacognitive skills in reflecting on their own revisions. If they are already oriented to the revision process, this will help them blend this practice in without much discomfort.

In the previous chapter we were guided by the "Make Them Revise It" map. I have the students revise for grammar until after they have mastered the revision procedure, including metacognition. As soon as they are comfortable enough completing the revision tasks I outlined in chapter four, I add sentence-level craft into the revision process. I have found this is the time when the learning sticks the most. Without further ado, on the following page you will find the same map from chapter four with sentence-level craft practice added into the process and written in bold:

THE "MAKE THEM REVISE IT" MAP (+ Craft)	
Step	**Task**
1	Write a number of entries in the Writer's Notebook
2	The students choose an entry to revise
3	They plan their revisions by annotating their chosen entry with the revision tool you have chosen
4	**The students choose two sentence-level craft elements to include in their second draft and write them out in the margin of their first draft entry.**

5	The students use the plan to write the next draft (consider using the Meta-Margin)
6	The students highlight the changes they made when writing their second drafts
7	The students hold writing conversations about the changes made, taking notes on their thinking.
8	**The students identify the two sentence-level craft elements and label each part of their sentences according to the checklist.**
9	The students record their metacognition and make it visible, writing it in the margin of their second draft.
10	The students submit their work.

To blend in this practice, you will need to expand your scoring guide checklist (Appendix E). Give the checklist to the students *before* they start planning their second drafts. Giving it to them upfront allows them to better plan their sentence-level craft revisions/additions. I have also created PowerPoint slideshows for implementing this part of the process. I invite you to download these files at https://makethemmasterit.com/mtpi-dropbox/. Again, feel free to modify the slideshows to fit your teaching style and personality. There is only one condition I ask as you use them: do not modify content of the final slide.

Corrections: Make Them Pinpoint Their Craft Issues

When the students submit their second draft entries with their metacognition made visible, their sentence-craft labeled, and their checklists filled out, this is when I assess and score their work. It is very easy to spot errors because, if they did not label their work correctly, the mislabeled elements will stand out. This makes awarding points a quick and simple task. At times I have completed a class set in the waning minutes of a class period, when my students are finishing up an assignment I have given them.

When I notice that students have incorrectly labeled, or completely misidentified, their chosen element of sentence-craft, I don't want to miss a teachable moment. First off, students who commit an error on the sentence-craft will not earn any points. So I will pinpoint the error for them and give them an opportunity to go back and fix the error. I give them a correction sheet, which has a checklist, that guides them through pinpointing the error. When they make the correction, they will recover their points.

Once they have pinpointed the error, I have them complete a brief handout going over the concept they are missing. I won't prescribe a grammar curriculum here. If you have one you already use, I recommend you stick with that. The students will pick up the worksheet, learn a little more about the skill that causes them confusion, and complete it. Then they will go back to the correction sheet they were initially given and write another draft of their sentence-craft, correcting the labels.

The kinds of student errors come in three versions. First, they completely miss the sentence-craft. They choose one from page 2 of the scoring guide checklist (see Appendix E), they write down a sentence, and submit the assignment with their fingers crossed that they got it right. These are the easiest to spot, but sometimes the most difficult to figure out how to best help the maturing writer. Second, the students made an error in writing the element of sentence-craft. For instance, if they claimed they were writing a compound sentence, but did not include a comma when it was needed, then they made an error. These kinds of errors are easiest for students to grasp and fix. Last, they produce an excellently written sentence, but they do not label the parts correctly. This error tells me that they can intuit how a particular grammar rule functions, but they have yet to understand it. I want to help them understand *how* writing works, so I make them go back to their sentences to learn more about the concepts that lie behind the grammar rule.

To date, this is the best process I am aware of in getting students to make the connection between the craft and grammar they are learning in class to the writing they are producing. Many studies have shown that most students don't connect the skills learned in grammar lessons with their own writing. Usually grammar is one activity the students complete at one point of the class period and their writing is a completely separate activity they complete at another point. Students don't naturally make the jump from *learning* new grammar to *using* new grammar.

The process I am describing here may sound like an inconvenience for students--they go over their drafts several times, and now they are getting it back without points because of an error they made? But after repeated practice, they get to know the expectations of the assignment. For the most part, the majority of my students have taken it in stride. And the students who resist it at first end up growing tired of making the same errors. Eventually many students start asking me pinpointed questions about their grammar, "Is this a dependent clause," or "The comma goes before the coordinating conjunction in a compound sentence, right?" These questions show me they are taking the learning opportunities to heart. And some of my students have reported that the error corrections have been some of the best learning they have received in recent memory.

Caution: Don't Make Them Do Too Much at Once

A word of caution: I add in this layer of complexity, the sentence-craft requirement, after the students have developed their metacognitive and revision muscles a little bit. I wouldn't advise including the sentence-craft part of the process at the outset of teaching students the revision process. I have made the mistake of pushing the students to do metacognition and sentence-craft assessment simultaneously. It was a complex knot of confusion that took too much time to detangle. Learn from my mistakes. Work in the complexity in waves, just like wading into the ocean where the beach has a shallow grade.

I have included a sample learning progression that can help you think through how to integrate sentence-craft, while rolling out this whole process, in Appendix A.

Chapter 6 | Publication

Make Them Put It Out There

Professional writers, and even amateurs, have regular experience watching their writing go from concept to draft to published. It is important that students get a taste for seeing this process through to conclusion. There are many lessons I want my students to learn about writing, but one of the major lessons is that writing is a multi-step, multi-layered process. We all know that writers don't just cough up a piece of writing on the strength of some innate talent. The "spontaneous prose" movement ended when Jack Kerouac passed away. The reality for writers is that, like gardening, writing is the kind of thing that takes shape over time.

In this spirit I recommend, from time to time, you have the students publish their writing for everyone to see. And for this step--just like you made them write several first drafts, then choose one for revision--have the students complete several second drafts and then choose one for publishing. At the point when you introduce publishing into your overall classroom writing practice, they should have some decent revision skills under their belts, so the third draft will be done entirely on their own. That this next draft will be made public will be enough pressure to push the students to make their writing even better.

Give them an attractive template, or format, for the

students to display their content. In my experience, students complain about the ugly formatting of MLA. Give them a different way to present their published drafts. If you're not sure what to do, tap into the skillset of your classes and have a few motivated students come up with a design that looks good to students.

Prominent Posts: Make Them Celebrate

As you use the Writer's Notebook to drive your classroom writing instruction, students will produce more and better quality writing. You will see more of your students' writing as well, which means you will get more chances to read exemplary work. As you experience more of the good stuff, it would be wise to capture those and put them on display.

I have a wall of fame in my classroom where I display superlatives in writing: funniest line, most entertaining, deepest thinker, most heartfelt, etc. I will leave one labeled "Noteworthy" for a piece of writing where I see something worth celebrating. Last year, that was Giselle; she used a semicolon perfectly without teacher prompting. That earned her a spot on the wall!

Having a showcase of good student writing helps the class to see that there are great examples among their peers. You don't have to do superlatives like I do, but it is important to develop some kind of display for excellent student work. And make sure *it is* excellent. That means I sometimes have student examples that stay up on the wall for quite a while because in subsequent assignments, students did not raise the bar high enough. And that's okay. We don't always do our best work either. And that's why it is helpful to remember that *there is always the next draft!*

Identity: Make Them Believe They Are Writers

Even if some students don't make the showcase, it is still important they see themselves as writers--people who move writing from concepts and ideas to a draft, revise their work, and publish a final product. Aside from the showcase, put the final product of student work in a published form of some kind. It could go in a binder or folder, one that makes the students' published work look attractive.

One of the weekly practices in my classroom is time for outside reading. We will start three class periods a week with Sustained Silent Reading (SSR) where the students read a book of their choice. Sometimes the students forget to bring their book with them to class. I have a small classroom library they can choose from (not a book on their mobile device). I plan to slowly fill this shelf with student publications for those reluctant and forgetful readers who leave their books at home. They will choose to read their peers' work and it will reinforce the writing culture that I am developing in my classroom.

Reading other students' work will lead to dialogue. As the students share their published work, whether they volunteer or not, the reality of seeing themselves as writers will settle in. All of the practices in this book, if implemented together, have the potential to transform any classroom into a writer's workshop where writing is done, shared, discussed, and celebrated. Then what we know to be true about all students will come out: everyone has something worth saying.

Afterward

At this point, you are getting the picture that the Writer's Notebook can be the centerpiece a teacher can use to drive powerful writing instruction for his or her students. From helping students brainstorm their own subjects for writing, to writing that first draft, to making intentional choices in the revision process, and finishing their writing with a publication they can be proud of, the Writer's Notebook is the tool that can help students shift their writing identity. And it can do all of this without making them write essays.

Developing the practices I have detailed in this book weren't easy. They were hard fought. There are great resources out there about strategies to use in a Writer's Notebook, and they were a great help to me along the way. But I had yet to find someone to walk me through the process, from the beginning of the year to the end. I'm a visual person, and it's difficult for me to move forward without a clear picture of the journey before me, especially in teaching.

That's why I wrote this book. In full disclosure, I wrote it for me. I need this. But I know its value, and I wanted it to be available to others like me. It is helpful to see how an instructional tool can be used from start to finish. Having the experience of starting the Writer's Notebook and fizzling out enough times showed me that I needed to finish, and once I had that taste of getting through an entire year, I was hooked. I know this will be a practice I carry with me for the rest of my career.

Let me leave you with this. At the end of this past academic year, I had several students insisting that I let them keep their notebooks. Of course, that was the plan, but before the final day came, they wanted to make sure that they let me know they wanted that notebook. One student in particular remarked, "That's my life in there." When I handed it back to her, the final time it would pass from my hand to hers, she clutched it to her chest. It started as a 99 cent booklet of lined paper for her, but in the end it had become something priceless.

What if you could give a gift like that to your students? Just imagine.

APPENDICES

Appendix A

The Writer's Notebook Learning Progression

If you have arrived at this point having made the decision that you *will* use the Writer's Notebook in your classroom, great! Like me when I made the decision to use it, however, you probably don't know quite what it looks like to use it in the classroom. All you see is handing out the composition book, students writing in it, and maybe the pile of student writing that you will be reading through. It's not clear quite how it will fit in the flow of your academic year.

In this appendix, I will give you some thoughts about how to roll out each element of the Writer's Notebook in manageable steps. Keep in mind that what I am giving you here is *one way* to approach using this instructional tool. If you want to do something different, go for it! If you make it your own, I want to hear about it at my website *http://makethemmasterit.com*.

The School Calendar

Speaking as a high school teacher, my district's academic year is divided into two semesters, each 18 weeks in length. My goal in using the Writer's Notebook is to fill up as many of those weeks with writing as possible. To give my students enough of a buffer at key points in the semester, I plan to use 15 of the 18 weeks in each semester for the Writer's Notebook.

I have found the Writer's Notebook works best in three-week blocks. That means that I will be breaking down the instruction into five three-week blocks per semester. This will give me time at the start of the year as first semester ramps up to communicate requirements to students. It will also give me time in the middle of the semester if a break is needed. I want to give my students, and myself, enough breathing room so that their workload isn't too heavy or their calendars too crowded. And, even though I have the goal of 15 weeks of writing in their notebooks in mind, I am willing to let a couple of weeks go if something else happens to come up.

All the Elements

The Writer's Notebook will host the following:

- Student generated topic brainstorms
- Craft lessons
- Entries

Even though that is a short list, keep in mind all that the students will be doing with those pages:

1. Brainstorming writing topics
2. Drafting compositions
3. Taking notes on writing lessons

4. Planning revision
5. Engaging in writing conversations
6. Evaluating the quality of their writing
7. Practicing revising drafts
8. Typing drafts for publication
9. Reflecting on the writing process
10. Celebrating their growth as writers

It is impossible to introduce this all at once. The students wouldn't be able to take it all in! So I recommend rolling it out in manageable steps to maintain the integrity and unlock the potential of the Writer's Notebook.

Progressive Roll Out

Keeping three-week blocks in mind, here is how I suggest that we all wade into the full implementation of the Writer's Notebook:

- **Block 1: Introduce the notebook**
  - Students set up the notebook, labelling sections and numbering pages
  - Students begin to meet the challenge of writing to your length requirement
  - Have students brainstorm lists for topical themes
  - Introduce three simple sentence craft lessons

- **Block 2: Introduce Revision**
  - Continue practicing the elements from block 1
  - Introduce the revision tool of your choice (for me, that is RADaR)
  - Students begin the practice of planning for revision

- Once per week, students move one entry from a first to a second draft
- Students begin holding writing conversations & using the Meta-Margin
- Only teach two sentence craft lessons for writing (invest one week in teaching the revision tool)

- **Block 3: Introduce Publishing**
  - Continue practice from blocks 1 & 2
  - During the revision process, introduce the expectation that they will include the elements of craft that they have been learning and recording in their craft section
  - Continue the process of revising drafts
  - Have the students select one of their revised drafts to move to third draft for publication
    - Post exemplary work in prominent places
    - Place the rest of the students' publications in a binder to display

At this point you have fully immersed the students into the Writer's Notebook and how it will be used in your class. The challenge before you now is to maintain the novelty of each part of the process. What I mean is that you must keep the Writer's Notebook fresh for the students. If they go too long thinking that it's a drag, then it just becomes part of the noise of school work, one more thing they have to do. It needs to stay fresh for them, so think it through. Look at your school calendar. Look at your curriculum. Look at planned curriculum of other subject areas. Look at events going on in the world. Tap into student interests and needs, then make the Writer's Notebook a place where they process their world. This will make it indispensable to them, and you.

All pictures and files in this section of the book can be found at
https://makethemmasterit.com/mtpi-dropbox/

Appendix B

Three-Week, Compressed Writer's Notebook "Alongside Micro-Unit"

If you picked up a copy of this book at a point in the year where it wouldn't make sense to have your students pick up a composition book and start from the beginning, but you want to do *something*, this is the place to start. It's also a great place to begin if you want a way to test this idea without trying to reframe how you see your entire academic year.

What I am presenting here is what I am calling an "alongside micro-unit." This practice is not meant to usurp your curriculum. If done right, it can augment and support the curriculum you are currently working on. That being said, this is a compressed version of the entirety of the Writer's Notebook down into three weeks. So, find a good spot on the calendar to shoehorn in this "alongside micro-unit" because you will need to give it some focus.

Materials Needed

I recommend making this a project that students bundle and turn in all together as one packet. That way you can flip through it to see if you like the results. All of the recommendations here are made with that in mind. On the next page is a breakdown of the materials each student will need to complete this alongside micro-unit:

- Table of Contents: 1 piece of binder paper
- Notebook Entries: 8 pieces of binder paper
- Notes on revision tool of choice (I recommend RADaR): 1 piece of paper
- Sentence craft lessons: 2 pieces of binder paper
- Second draft writing: 3 pieces of binder paper
- Metacognition: highlighters (For those who use RADaR, use four colors)

Note: That's a total of 15 pages of binder paper.

Scope of the Writer's Notebook "Alongside Micro-Unit"

What follows is a rundown of what you can cover in the three-week "alongside micro-unit" and what you can cover each week. The design is to give the teacher an experience that is simple to navigate while painting a clear picture of what this could look like on a weekly basis. The themes selected below were also included for the sake of simplicity and ease.

- **Week 1**
  - Introduction to the "alongside micro-unit" (For your students, I recommend calling it a writing process project, since that's what they will be learning through it)
  - 5 entries by prompt (see list of prompt ideas)
  - Instruction and practice in your chosen revision tool

- 1 second draft of an entry (Meta-Margin recommended)
- Introduction to the metacognitive process - students make their thinking visible about changes made in revision of their first draft.

- **Week 2**
  - 5 entries by the rhetorical mode of narration
  - 1 sentence craft lesson (your choice, but I recommend 'complex sentences')
  - Continued practice using the revision tool
  - 1 second draft entry
  - Continued practice in the metacognitive process

- **Week 3**
  - 5 entries by the topical theme: Firsts
  - 1 sentence craft lesson (your choice, but I recommend 'compound sentences')
  - Continued practice using the revision tool
  - 1 second draft entry
  - Continued practice is the metacognitive process

- **Post-Week 3**
  - Students choose a revised entry to take through the revision process once again.
    - This final draft will be called "publication"
    - This part is on their own
  - Students submit publication typed and ready for display
    - I recommend coming up with an attractive format for their presentation
    - Display the best examples

- Keep the rest in a small binder to show off their writing

Possible Prompts

On the next page are some suggested prompts to get you started. If you think of something better suited for your classroom, you should use those instead.

Here's a list of prompts:

- Write about a memorable place (could be positive or negative).
- Write about a lesson learned (could be positive or negative).
- What makes a true friend?
- What are two videos, or channels on YouTube, everyone should watch? Why?
- How do you protect yourself from the evils of social media?
- What would change about life at school if studying suddenly became popular?
- How would things change if everyone you knew stopped cheating?
- What's one trend, or popular saying, that needs to "just stop"?

Rhetorical Mode: Narration

Other than description, this rhetorical mode is simple enough for students to understand because they have a lot of experience with it. And while you're figuring out how this all works, let's keep things as simple as possible.

With the rhetorical mode "theme" you are giving students parameters, but they are coming up with the subjects they will be writing about. Start the week by discussing and defining the elements of the rhetorical mode, then have them begin to build a list of topics (positive or negative) they can write about in this mode. You can narrow down the scope of their topics as much as you want, but keep in mind you want them to enjoy the writing for this assignment as much as possible.

If your students need the extra help thinking it through, you can write your own list before class and show it to them. This can help them come up with ideas. It's also an opportunity to connect with them as well, where students recognize that they may have something in common with you.

If you have an essay coming up, then you could have them practice writing anecdotes related to that topic. But if you're in the opposite situation, and you just finished up an essay, maybe you could have them go back and add an anecdote to punch up their introductions or to better illustrate an abstract point they were making.

Topical Theme: Firsts

Like the Rhetorical Mode theme, you are going to present the topic to the students and let them build a list of ten topics they can develop in 100-150 words of writing. Help them brainstorm the topic. You can present possible items by showing them your list, or you could verbally volley them as you walk the classroom while they are building their lists.

Here are some possible *firsts* to put out there:

- First day at this school.
- First kiss.
- First time I got in trouble at school.
- First time I tried Tapatio.
- My first cell phone.
- The first thing I do when I get home from school.
- The first website/app I check every day.

Sequence of the "Alongside Micro-Unit"

Below I lay out the compressed version of everything in this book with references to earlier sections of the book if you need to review for further guidance. For the purpose of more focus from your students, I recommend starting day 1 of each week on a Wednesday, which you will see indicated in the plan below.

Week 1 (writing from prompts):

- **Day 1** (Wed):
  o Introduce "alongside micro-unit"
  o 10 minutes writing from a prompt
  o Transition to previously planned content

- **Day 2** (Thur):
  o 10 minutes writing from a prompt
  o Lesson on Revision Tool (I recommend RADaR, introduced in chapter 4)
    ■ Remember to teach that this is time to think like a reader.

- What will make your second draft, if you write one, a better read?
  - Practice Revision Tool on one of the entries
    - My students practice RADaR on 3 entries a week.
    - They practice whether they move to a second draft or not.
  - If time permits, transition to previously planned content

- **Day 3** (Fri):
  - 10 minutes writing from a prompt
  - Review and practice revision on entry
  - Transition to previously planned content

- **Day 4** (Mon):
  - 10 minutes writing from a prompt
  - Review and practice revision tool
  - Students select the entry they want to see move to a second draft
    - Prescribe the elements you want them to revise
    - For instance, I will tell my students I want to see 2 replacements, 2 additions, 1 deletion, and 1 re-ordered element (phrase, sentence, or paragraph).
  - Transition to previously planned content
                    -OR-
  - Have the students write their second draft
    - I recommend using the Meta-Margin (Chapter 4)
    - The added space the right will give them the room they need for writing their metacognition.

- **Day 5** (Tues):
  - 10 minutes writing from a prompt

- I recommend having the students have a writing conversation (Chpater 4) here, but if you are pressed for time you can simply have them move on to writing about their thinking
- Students highlight the changes they made from their first to their second draft
- Students write out their metacognition in the margins
  - Why did you make this change?
  - Why do you think that will make your entry better reading?
- Students submit their second drafts
- If time permits, transition to previously planned content

Week 2 (writing from a rhetorical mode - narration):

- **Day 1** (Wed):
  - Introduce the rhetorical mode of narration
    - Ask students to make a list of ten events/circumstances they could write a story about.
    - Briefly teach them what an anecdote is
    - Mention the stories can be funny, sad, happy, exciting, etc.
  - 10 minutes of writing from the mode of narration
  - Deliver sentence-craft lesson, students take notes
  - Transition to previously planned content

- **Day 2** (Thur):
  - 10 minutes of writing from the mode of narration
  - Practice using the revision tool
  - Transition to previously planned content

- **Day 3** (Fri):
  - 10 minutes of writing from the mode of narration
  - Practice using the revision tool
  - Transition to previously planned content

- **Day 4** (Mon):
  - 10 minutes of writing from the mode of narration
  - Plan revision - the students choose which entry they will move to a second draft
  - Students begin writing the second draft (Meta-Margin recommended)
  - Transition to previously planned content

- **Day 5** (Tues):
  - 10 minutes of writing from the mode of narration
  - Students take out second drafts and begin the metacognitive process
  - Students submit their second draft entries
  - If time permits, transition to previously planned content

Week 3 (writing from a topic theme):

- **Day 1** (Wed):
  - Introduce students to the topical theme: Firsts
    - Have students make a list of ten 'firsts' they have experienced
    - Help them brainstorm by showing them a list you have made
    - It could be their first time moving, first time they tried a new food, or their first kiss (those are usually very entertaining reads).

- 10 minutes of writing from the topical theme: Firsts
- Deliver sentence craft lesson, students take notes.
- Transition to previously planned content

- **Day 2** (Thur):
  - 10 minutes of writing from the topical theme: Firsts
  - Students practice using the revision tool
  - Transition to previously planned content

- **Day 3** (Fri):
  - 10 minutes of writing from the topical theme: Firsts
  - Students practice using the revision tool
  - Transition to previously planned content

- **Day 4** (Mon):
  - 10 minutes of writing from the topical theme: Firsts
  - Plan revision - the students choose which entry they will move to a second draft
  - New this week, give them the scoring guide checklist
    - The students are adding an element to their revision
    - The students must include a sentence for each craft lesson previously taught
    - They must correctly identify each part of the craft.
  - Students begin writing the second draft (Meta-Margin recommended)
  - Transition to previously planned content

- **Day 5** (Tues):
  - 10 minutes of writing from the topical theme: Firsts
  - Students take out second drafts and begin the metacognitive process
  - Students submit their second draft entries

- ○ If time permits, transition to previously planned content

Post-Week 3:

- Within a week of the students submitting their third second draft, hand back all three second drafts.
- Ask the students to choose one to move to publication
- Ask them to revise it again, but this time it is on their own
- Give them a reasonable timeframe to complete a typed draft
- Collect and put together in some bound form (a binder or folder) and post the best examples for all to see

All pictures and files in this section of the book can be found at
https://makethemmasterit.com/mtpi-dropbox/

Appendix C

Revision Read Aloud Guide

Here is the sheet used to guide the students through their paired writing conversations:

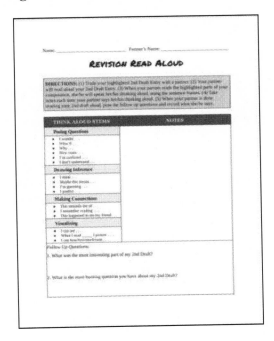

The link that follows will take you to a downloadable version of this file. Make it your own.

All pictures and files in this section of the book can be found at
https://makethemmasterit.com/mtpi-dropbox/

Appendix D

RADaR Revision Sentence Stems

REVISION METACOGNITION--SENTENCE STEMS	

Directions: Use these sentence stems to take the thinking behind your revision choices, and make it visible.

REPLACE (RP)	
SURFACE-LEVEL REVISION	**DEEP-LEVEL REVISION**
Better word	**Changed the focus of the writing.**
➤ "_____ was a better word than _____ because . . ."	➤ "I replaced _____ with this text because the first draft communicated _____ when really I want to get across that . . ."
Clarity - Made the sentence clearer	**Clarity - Made the whole piece clearer**
➤ "Replacing the word/phrase _____ with _____ made the sentence clearer because . . ."	➤ "I replaced my first example/story of _____ and replaced it with this example/story to make it more clear that . . ."
➤ "My original sentence was _____, so I made it clearer by . . ."	
Too abstract/concrete	
➤ "_____ was too abstract, so I replaced it with _____ which better specifies . . ."	
➤ "_____ was too concrete, so I replaced it with _____ which broadens the idea of . . ."	
Avoid repetition	
➤ "I replaced _____ with _____ because I already used that word/phrase in . . ."	

ADD (A)	
SURFACE-LEVEL REVISION	**DEEP-LEVEL REVISION**
Details	**Added significant development**
➤ "I added _____ because it was needed to make it clear that . . ."	➤ "I discovered that the idea of _____ was too big for one paragraph, so I added another to be sure to communicate . . ."
➤ "The paragraph was missing the key detail _____ which helped . . ."	➤ "My writing need more _____, so I added the anecdote about _____ to liven up the point about . . ."
Needed information	➤ "The idea of _____ wasn't clear on its own, so I added the explanation about _____ to show . . ."
➤ "_____ need to be added because, without _____, it wouldn't be clear that . . ."	➤ "My point about _____ was unclear, so I added the illustration _____ to paint the picture that . . ."
Descriptive adjective/adverb	➤ "My first draft felt like it needed more context, so I added _____ in order to . . ."
➤ "The word _____ was missing something, so I added the adjective _____ to communicate . . ."	
➤ "The verb _____ wasn't specific enough, so I added the adverb _____ to show . . ."	
Rhetorical/literary device	
➤ "I added the rhetorical/literary device _____ to better illustrate the point that . . ."	
➤ "The repetition of _____ was added in order to emphasize . . ."	
➤ "The metaphor/simile of _____ helps connect _____ with the idea that . . ."	

DELETE (D)

SURFACE-LEVEL REVISION	DEEP-LEVEL REVISION

SURFACE-LEVEL REVISION

Unnecessary repetition

➤ "I took out _____ because I already wrote that in . . ."
➤ "I noticed I was writing _____ too many times and it made my writing sound . . ."

Extra details

➤ "I deleted the word/phrase/clause/sentence because . . ."

Too descriptive

➤ "The word _____ carried enough meaning, so I took out _____ because it was unnecessary"
➤ "The verb _____ precisely communicated _____, so I deleted _____."

Awkward phrasing

➤ "_____ made the sentence sound _____, so I got rid of it"
➤ "Writing _____ made the sentence sound _____."

DEEP-LEVEL REVISION

Distracting or vague details/information

➤ "The word/phrase _____ worked, but it didn't the overall _____ tone because . ."
➤ "The word/phrase _____ didn't connect to the rest of the paragraph about _____, so I deleted it."
➤ "The word/phrase _____ overemphasized my point about _____. Taking it out made the draft more . . "
➤ "The word/phrase _____ miscommunicated that _____. Deleting it made the paragraph . . "

REORDER (RO)

SURFACE-LEVEL REVISION	DEEP-LEVEL REVISION

SURFACE-LEVEL REVISION

Flow

➤ "Moving the word _____ from the _____ to the _____ made the sentence read better because . . ."
➤ "The phrase _____ worked better at the _____ of the sentence than at the _____ because . . ."
➤ "I reordered the words in the sentence because . . ."

Sequence of details

➤ "When I reordered the details to _____, _____, and _____ they better communicated the point that . . ."
➤ "Moving _____ in the list made better sense because . . ."
➤ "This detail fit better in paragraph # _ rather than paragraph # _ because . . ."

Combined sentences

➤ "The ideas of _____ and _____ in each sentence were so closely related, I decided to combine them by _____ because . . ."
➤ "To better show the _____ between each sentence, I combined them with _____ "

Uncombined sentences

➤ "The sentence had two ideas: _____ and _____. I decided to separate them because . . ."
➤ "The point about _____ was better emphasized in a simple sentence, so I seperated it from . . ."

DEEP-LEVEL REVISION

Bed-to-bed writing

➤ "My first draft didn't highlight the exciting detail about _____, so I moved it to the _____ because . . ."
➤ "I deleted _____ and moved the detail about _____ up to _____ in order to . . ."

Sequence

➤ "Paragraph # _ in my first draft fits better at the beginning because . . ."
➤ "Paragraph # _ in my first draft fits better in the middle because . . ."
➤ "Paragraph # _ in my first draft fits better at the end because . . ."

All pictures and files in this section of the book can be found at
https://makethemmasterit.com/mtpi-dropbox/

Appendix E

Scoring Guide Checklist

Page 1

I roll out the students revision instruction in layers. First, I get the students in the habit of looking at the writing a second time with basic revision and proofreading. The Scoring Guide Checklist starts at the simplest level and then grows as the year progresses. This checklist is turned in upon review of their second draft. Page 1 will take them through basic proofreading and the metacognitive moves they were asked to make when they reviewed their 2nd Draft Entry.

Here's what page 1 looks like:

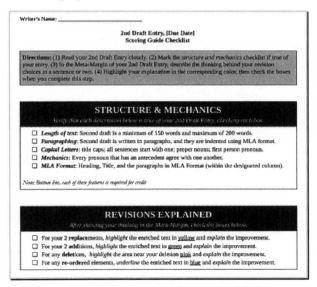

Writer's Name: _____

2nd Draft Entry, [Due Date]
Scoring Guide Checklist

Directions: (1) Read your 2nd Draft Entry closely. (2) Mark the *structure and mechanics* checklist if true of your entry. (3) In the Meta-Margin of your 2nd Draft Entry, describe the thinking behind your revision choices in a sentence or two. (4) Highlight your explanation in the corresponding color, then check the boxes when you complete this step.

STRUCTURE & MECHANICS
Verify that each description below is true of your 2nd Draft Entry, checking each box.

- ☐ **Length of text:** Second draft is a minimum of 150 words and maximum of 200 words.
- ☐ **Paragraphing:** Second draft is written in paragraphs, and they are indented using MLA format.
- ☐ **Capital Letters:** title caps; all sentences start with one; proper nouns; first person pronoun.
- ☐ **Mechanics:** Every pronoun that has an antecedent agree with one another.
- ☐ **MLA Format:** Heading, Title, and the paragraphs in MLA Format (within the designated column).

Note: Bottom line, each of these features is required for credit

REVISIONS EXPLAINED
After showing your thinking in the Meta-Margin, check the boxes below.

- ☐ For your 2 **replacements**, *highlight* the enriched text in yellow and *explain* the improvement.
- ☐ For your 2 **additions**, *highlight* the enriched text in green and *explain* the improvement.
- ☐ For any **deletions**, *highlight* the area near your deletion pink and *explain* the improvement.
- ☐ For any **re-ordered** elements, *underline* the enriched text in blue and *explain* the improvement.

Page 2

After the students have developed some muscle memory in basic proofreading and the metacognitive demands placed on their 2nd Draft Entry, I add another layer to the revision process. The students need to be aware that they will be held accountable for this *before* they begin planning their 2nd Draft Entries.

What you see on the following page is a snapshot of what I give to the students:

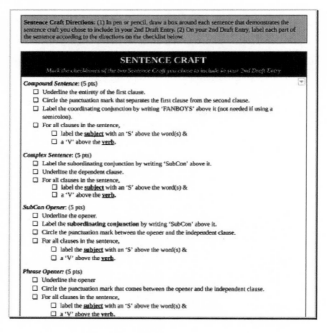

Page 2 is always open for revision. I would like to give you the file that has both pages; download it and make it your own. Use symbols and labels that make sense to you. If you come up with something brilliant, then let me know about it at https://makethemmasterit.com.

All pictures and files in this section of the book can be found at
https://makethemmasterit.com/mtpi-dropbox/

About The Author

Jeffery E. Frieden is a full-time high school English Language Arts teacher in Southern California, where he has been teaching for the past 13 years. Other than working closely with his students to improve their writing, he has enjoyed working closely with colleagues at the high school and college level to better improve his grasp of what students need to be college and career ready readers and writers.

He lives in the City of Ontario with his talented and beautiful wife (@lindseyspalette on Instagram) and their three kids. You can follow him on Twitter at @MakeThemMastrIt or swing by his growing website https://makethemmasterit.com for posts and conversations about the trials and joys of teaching English Language Arts.

Made in the USA
San Bernardino, CA
28 July 2018